Seth

THE NATURE OF GOD

THE NATURE OF GOD

B.B. Dandekar

GYAN

ISBN: 978-81-212-1227-4

Price: ₹ 450

First Published, 2014

Published by

Gyan Publishing House
23, Main Ansari Road
Daryaganj, New Delhi-110002
Phones: 23282060, 23261060
Fax: 91-11-23285914
E-mail: books@gyanbooks.com

Laser Typesetting: Gyan Print (AB-I)

Printed at: Chawla Offset Printers, Delhi

Cataloging in Publication Data--DK

Courtesy: D.K. Agencies (P) Ltd. <docinfo@dkagencies.com>

Dandekar, B. B.

The nature of god / B.B. Dandekar.

p. cm.
ISBN 9788121212274

1. God-Proof, Cosmological. 2. Faith. I. Title.

DDC 231 23

Contents

Preface

This book is a conversation between you and me. Yes, you—who are turning it over in your hand in a bookstore, wondering whether it is worth buying, or, perhaps, looking at it on a bookshelf in your local library, wondering whether you ought to waste your time reading it, or, perhaps, buying it at the annual library sale, wondering whether it will fit into the $1 grocery bag, if you ease it in. I don't know who you are; male or female, old or young, blue collar or white collar or no collar. You don't know who I am. It does not matter. Because, what interests us both is the search for the truth about the last great mystery of our time—the nature of God.

We—you and I—are sitting at a small, round table in an open air café, sharing a glass of wine—or beer, or tea, or coffee, for you if you wish. But the sidewalk café is really an open air courtroom at the center of the universe. Our court of inquiry is open to all. Every discipline that has evidence to offer will be welcome to stand before us and tell us—in simple language—their telling stories.

God is not on trial! I am neither his defense attorney nor his prosecutor. You are not the jury. All we would like to hear is the evidence. What say you? Shall we?

B.B. Dandekar

A Courtroom on the Sidewalk

I am sitting at a small, round table tucked away in one corner of a sidewalk café, waiting for you to come—not knowing whether you will come. Behind me is the open window of the café, but I am oblivious to the noise and bustle of the goings and comings of customers, who are dropping in for breakfast or a cup of coffee. I have ordered my cup of tea, with a little milk and sugar, British style. Later, perhaps, I will order a glass of white wine—a Riesling, if they have it—and then sit down to watch the traffic go by on this side street off the downtown area. As you may have guessed by now, I have time on my hands—to watch the traffic go by.

Occasionally the café owner's wife or daughter—who are helping him to run the café—will come out and inquire if I need anything—a refill of my tea cup or more paper napkins? I blurt out my apologies for having occupied their table with so meager a fare—a cup of tea, and the promise of a glass of wine, later—but she gently waves it away.

Sit, she says. Passersby see the table occupied, and that is good for business! I'll talk to my husband in the café. We'll see you are not disturbed.

You slide into the seat beside me, with your cup of hot, black coffee. No sugar; no milk.

You wanted to talk. Well, I am here. So talk!

1

Three Types of Belief in God

Many people believe in God. I know I do. And in the power of prayer. Anyone who has teenage children, in a car, out late at night, in icy weather conditions, and more than two hours overdue, without a phone call of reassurance, knows precisely what I mean.

But the way in which we think about God, beseech him, implore him, thank him when the doorbell rings and we hear the apologetic, loving voices at the door, or castigate him in moments of anger when he fails us—only to return to him to apologise for our thoughtlessness and lack of understanding and plead for forgiveness in all this we may disagree. To some, God is precisely that. Someone to turn to, in times of desperate need. Someone who grants us favours and wishes, rescues us from danger, keeps us and our loved ones from harm, watches over us and protects us. In return, we try to be good and keep our faith in him. In some of us that faith is steadfast, unshakeable, constantly held, regardless of the trials and tribulations that beset our path—and we do believe he sets them before us to test our faith in him. In others, the faith is more human. It is reaffirmed at times, when the events in our lives make it very clear he has come to our aid; reaching to low levels of fickleness when it becomes abundantly clear that he has abandoned us.

To others, God is merely a sort of curiosity, a philosophical abstraction that permits the logical mind to find explanations that would otherwise be very hard to come by. We use him to explain that which we cannot otherwise explain. And in doing so, we shift onto his shoulders—as creator and sustainer—responsibility for all that we do not understand. Not so much responsibility and blame—because the philosophic mind does not attribute blame—but reasons, without which that same philosophic mind would find itself in a quagmire of argument, so wordy and involved that living in a state institution becomes an attractive alternative for saner thinking!

Where did this universe come from?

God created it.

Why did he create it?

His purpose has not been revealed to us. But that does not mean he doesn't have one!

Are you quite sure he created the universe?

Well, if he didn't, then who did? Answer that smart guy!

I don't have an answer either. But at least, I don't pretend to have one.

You guys are all the same! Just argue for the sake of arguing. Now, either you come up with a better argument than mine or shut up, before I end up pulling the last few hairs on my almost bald pate!

And then there is the scientific mind. Trained and open-minded. Orderly! Willing to accept only that which can be proved. Cause and effect! He must, like any other formula, be scientifically proven, discovered by theory and recorded by instruments—or otherwise he is unacceptable. If he wishes to be accepted, he must submit to being recorded, analysed, perhaps even being partially synthesised in a laboratory. All else is fiction.

Except when the scientific mind arrives at facts—such as the presence and origins of this universe, and the reasons why it should exist at all—that are not explainable by scientific theory, when it quite simply retreats into ignorance as its only line of defense.

A scientific explanation will, one day, be available. There is no reason to assume that it will not. Science will one day conquer all!

And there you have it. Three minds. Three different minds.

The religious mind. Able to feel. Satisfied by feeling alone. Total acceptance in humility. And unable to understand.

The philosophic mind. Probing through thought. Arriving at dead-ends in a logic that betrays itself. And unable to understand.

The scientific mind. Unwilling to accept that which cannot be proved. Laying down rigid rules of scientific method to obtain such proof. Boxed in by its own walls. And still unable to understand!

Even the attitudes to the same problem are different.

The religious mind has a humble attitude in probing the nature of God. There is no questioning; rather there is an acceptance that we are not really expected to know, and that when the time is appropriate, and of his choosing, both God and his purpose will be revealed to us. Such things cannot be forced! And in the infinite nature of timeless existence, a few billion years are less than a drop in the ocean.

The philosophic mind is confused and in agony. It wants to know. It seeks out conflicting paths of partial knowledge to enter a maze of its own design, without the master hand of total knowledge to guide it. The result? A series of unconnected half—truths that would have twelve-year-olds rollicking with laughter. Ah! But we'd better keep the twelve-year-olds out of this, and to do so we'll throw in such verbiage that the subject matter can never be part of a middle school curriculum. Geez! They'd split their sides with laughter, asking the teacher to put what she'd said in plain English! And what if she couldn't?

But the scientific mind takes the prize for arrogance. Would you care to tell me, please, how this universe can be finite but unbounded?

That needs higher mathematics. Besides Einstein says so.

Do you understand what Einstein says?

Not all of it. But more than you do, or you wouldn't ask such silly questions!

The scientific mind can, however, sometimes relent; condescend to stoop to my level.

Look. Can you imagine an ant walking on the surface of a bowling ball? Imagine you are the ant.

Yes; okay.

Well, the ant would continuously crawl round and around it. And it would say: This world of mine is unbounded! But of course we know that the bowling ball is finite! So, too, is the universe.

I am not an ant. I know that the bowling ball is contained within something else—which is space.

Within what do you contain space? For the same analogy to apply to the universe, you will need an envelope within which that space is contained for it to be boundless but finite. I don't understand it.

Ah! But to understand that, you need higher mathematics!

I didn't know mathematics had a class system in it? Isn't what I did in High School good enough anymore to understand the mysteries of the universe? Am I not an educated person?

I'm afraid not! You've been left far behind. Why don't you try gardening instead, and leave the mysteries of the universe—and the nature of God—to scientists who are better trained than you are. You see, you are the common man. Woman too. I have it! You are the common person!

And there we have it. We are the common people. Educated—or so we thought. Eager to learn. Very willing to accept. To be convinced by their religious, philosophic or scientific truths as they see them. More than willing to bend the intellectual mind to see figures in the shadows, when they tell us such figures exist, whereas all we can really see is a vibrant darkness. But we are unwilling to be swept aside as so ignorant or so stupid that philosophers and scientists wink knowingly at each other when we ask the questions we ask.

Is it because we ask the questions we ask?

We have a stubborn streak in us, we common people. We will still persist in asking questions and probe for answers, even if all the evidence isn't in and all the answers are not available.

This court of inquiry we hold will be open to all. Every discipline that has an argument to advance or a contribution to make will be welcome to come before us and tell us—in simple language—their compelling stories. Physics, astronomy, chemistry, biochemistry, microbiology, mathematics, evolutionary biology, entomology, neurology, psychology, the arts, poetry, dance, song and music that excites the soul—all will give their evidence on the last great remaining mystery of this or all time.

The nature of God.

2

The Origins of the Universe

This is a court of inquiry; not a trial. God is not on trial before us. That would be blasphemy! But I feel quite sure that if he exists and can hear us, he is with us in this courtroom today, listening with as much eagerness, as us, to the evidence that will be put before this court. And I feel equally sure that he will not sway our judgment nor influence our verdict when all of the available evidence is in and the time for closing argument and summation is upon us.

You said: If he exists! Does that mean that his very existence is in doubt?

Naturally. We have to receive evidence of it. Like everything else, we need evidence, do we not?

Is that too not blasphemy?

To some, maybe.

Denying his very existence before the case has even come to this court?

No! No! I did not deny his existence. Nor did I deny his non-existence. We will keep an open mind. There is one difference though between this court of inquiry and any other ever held. There will be no judge, sitting with the wisdom of his years, to guide us in what that verdict ought to be; no directives on points of law that clarify the issues for common people like us. Each person's verdict has to be a personal one. In that respect, this court of inquiry is unlike any mystery novel. In those novels, when all the evidence is in, the pieces of the jigsaw fall, sometimes tumultuously, into place, the total picture is very clearly delineated for everyone to read and see, and the arguments of the protagonist—which are the words of the writer—are indisputable.

Not, so here.

All the evidence will certainly not be in—and may never be in! Not only are pieces of the jigsaw puzzle missing, but we are not entirely sure that the puzzle itself does not stretch into three, four, or five dimensions, outside the range of our meager human comprehension! A puzzle in a single plane, placed on a flat table, and with some pieces missing, would be challenging. But with logic and imagination we might triumphantly slap each other on the back, with perhaps reasonably close alternative solutions. But if that same puzzle, with the pieces missing, then twists and curves and warps into other dimensions, we may well ask each other for some pity at the end!

That is why each person's verdict has to be a personal one. At the end, I will draw mine; you must draw yours. In some areas, where the evidence is strong or more complete, why, we may even be close to one another. And when that happens there will be that look of understanding between us and a warmth neither would like to admit. At other times, each will feel the coldness of the other's intellectual disdain, arising from the gnawing uncertainty that each of us is seeing his or her (I am a man, but you could be a woman) own truths, while looking into a black hole!

Where shall we begin?

At the beginning of course. With creation—if indeed there was one.

Are you denying that we exist? If you wrote this book and I am reading it, we must both exist, must we not? So something has been created. Are you denying that?

No. Not at all. But the actual act of creation has not been proven. No evidence has been admitted to that effect. So let us call in the physicist and the astronomer. They, more than anyone else, may throw some light on the actual act of creation.

There are two theories on the origins of the universe. One is the Steady State theory; the other is the Big Bang. Some are proponents of one theory; others of the other. So we will have to take evidence from both sides.

Now, wait a minute! There is yet another theory of the act of creation. The beginnings of the universe! The Judeo—Christian religious explanation that so many believe in. Why are you excluding them from giving evidence as to the creation of the universe?

Well said! We will not exclude anybody. You are right. We will invite them too, after we hear from the physicists and the astronomers. Above all, we will be fair and just. There is no room for bigotry in this court!

Now you're talking! Bring on the Steady State guy.

The Steady State theory finds that the universe has always existed. There is no beginning and no end. Since the universe has always been there, there is no single act of creation. But this theory that removes the question of what existed before creation, runs into conflict with some of the astronomical observations of the universe.

The astronomer tells us that we have an expanding universe, with the galaxies flying away from each other at incredible speeds. How do we know that? Because of the work of an Austrian scientist, Christian Doppler. He showed that sound waves emanating from one body and received by another, suffer a change in wavelength depending on the relative motion between them. If the two bodies are moving toward each other, the wavelength shortens; if the bodies are moving away from each other, the wavelength lengthens.

Prove it.

Prove it?

Yes! You don't expect me to accept your scientific claptrap, without relating it to my common experience, do you now? You said the evidence would be in plain English! Do I have to be a physics professor too?

Touche! Tell me, have you ever stood on a railway platform and listened to a fast train that is going to thunder past you, without stopping, threatening to tear the platform apart, blowing its whistle with a majesty of haste, warning you to stay away from the edge?

Yes.

Have you noticed that the pitch of the whistle rises as the train is approaching you; dies down as the train is moving away from you?

Yes! Yes!

Well, that is the Doppler Effect. Doppler showed it for sound waves, but it is true for light waves as well. For light waves, when bodies move toward each other, the wavelength shifts to the blue side of the spectrum; when they fly away from each other, the wavelength shifts to the red side of the spectrum.

And? Why are you keeping me in suspense?

And the light that is coming to us from the galaxies shows a shift to the red side of the spectrum. Like spots on an expanding balloon, all the galaxies are moving away from each other at fantastic speeds. We have an expanding universe! Hubble showed that the speed at which the galaxies are racing away from our own—the Milky Way—depended on the distance from us. His law, appropriately called Hubble's Law, was correct, though his calculations were not because of the difficulty he had in estimating the correct distances between galaxies. Present day calculations give the speed of the galaxy as being 10 per cent of the speed of light for every one billion light—years away. Since Einstein showed that the speed of light, at 186,282 miles per second in a vacuum, is the ultimate speed that can never be exceeded in the universe, it follows that the present size of the universe is about 10 billion light-years.

May I ask a question of the astronomer?

You can ask anything you wish. Of-course anyone!

What is a light-year?

The distance traveled by a beam of light, at that speed, in one year. You have to say that for scientists. They do try to simplify their language, so that it becomes intelligible to common people such as us! That distance—a light-year—can even be calculated as:

$186{,}282 \times 60 \times 60 \times 24 \times 365.25 = 5.9$ million miles.

And ten billion of them give us the present size of the universe.

But what is beyond the known universe? Into what is space expanding?

Into nothingness!

Then the entire universe may eventually, finally, be dissipated into infinite nothingness?

Yes. And that is why the Steady State theory, if it assumes, as its name implies, that a steady state of affairs has existed for eternal time and will exist for eternal time, is forced to the conclusion that matter and energy are being constantly produced in the universe to keep the distribution of matter and energy constant, consistent with a 'steady state' of affairs.

Well, what's wrong with that? So matter and energy are constantly being produced somewhere at the center of the universe.

That is precisely what is wrong with it! A theory that chose to bypass the question of the first act of creation, by telling us that the universe has always existed, is now forced to the conclusion that, in fact, creation is taking place all the time!

It is possible that the laws of physics that we deduce from our observations on Earth and in the heavens, may not apply to other regions of the universe. I think they do. And the Laws of Conservation tell us that matter and energy can be neither created nor destroyed. Matter can be transformed into energy—as in the atomic bomb—but the sum total of all the matter and energy in the universe is always a constant. New creation cannot occur.

With present day telescopes, we are able to receive information from as long ago as eight billion light years—almost the outer edge of the universe. There is not one shred of evidence that either matter or energy is being created anywhere.

What is particularly gratifying is the conclusion that astronomers have reached that, provided we look deep enough into space, our view of the universe is precisely the same as anyone else's view of the universe! For the first time we are seeing the complete picture of the universe—dwarfs, quasars, black holes, supernovas, and the galaxies that contain them—and no signs of new creation anywhere!

Creation transcends the Laws of Physics in our universe.

So much for the Steady State theory. I hope we did not offend him or hurt his feelings. He seemed so very sure of himself and his theory and his beliefs.

Not to worry! Isn't that the purpose of this inquiry? To question not only the beliefs of others but also our own? We have done him no harm. He will react in either of two ways. He might change his point of view, discard the theories he has held for so long, and find others that prove more intellectually satisfying. Or he will cling to his old beliefs, refine his instruments, sharpen his mathematical theories, and look deeper into space for that one spot in the universe where the Laws of Conservation do not apply and where, at this very moment, matter and energy are being constantly created out of nothingness!

And if he finds such a place in the universe, he may well have found God or, at the very least, an eternal fountain.

The other theory of the origins of the universe is the 'Big Bang'. The name was coined by opponents of the theory—in derogatory derision; not awe—but it stuck, and is now in common usage. As its name implies, it theorises that the universe came into being as a result of a large, cataclysmic explosion of overwhelming proportions that set the universe in motion, which motion continues to this day.

And they have proof of all this?

Yes. Though it is a little shaky, and though they will waffle in their answers to one question we will pose to them, they do make sense.

According to the theory, at the beginning of time, all of the matter and energy in the universe—all the millions of galaxies containing trillions of stars and including all interstellar matter—was energy contained in a very small volume. How small? Perhaps, the size of an apple. As can be understood, all of that energy compacted into such a small volume must have resulted in enormous internal pressures of unbelievable magnitude, resulting in a horrendous explosion as the universe came into being. It took only fractions of a second, but in that very short time, our universe was born. The initial act of creation had been completed. Nothing would be the same any more. With an estimated temperature of ten billion degrees, and hurtling radiation rocketing, at incredible speeds approaching the speed of light, into space on their long and still continuing journey, it must have been an awesome sight, witnessed, perhaps, by only the one spectator. And the only witness to it. Oh! That we could call on him for his evidence! How would he have described it? As a wanton act of godly capriciousness or of frustration? Or some godly vanity as a display of power?

Or was it a carefully planned, very well-thought out, perfectly orchestrated act with purpose and meaning? The start of a meaningful progression of events, with every law of physics first instituted into place, so that every burning neutron or spinning electron released in the maelstrom knew precisely what it was supposed to do?

Who can say?

But happen it did. Even the time and the place can be identified.

The time when it occurred?

At most, about thirteen billion years ago. Not too long ago in the measure of infinite time. That lasts forever! It could have happened only yesterday.

And the place?

At a spot in the universe about ten billion light-years away.

And how do they arrive at that science-fiction spot, may I ask?

You certainly may. Do you remember the receding galaxies that are hurtling away from each other, as on the surface of an expanding balloon?

Yes, I do.

Well, all that the astronomers did was to trace the path of each galaxy backward to determine where it started from, and, surprisingly, they found that all of these lines intersect at a point in the universe. A single point! The point from which they all took off on their separate journeys into space. The point of creation!

Those who believe in the theory of the Big Bang believe in an act of creation at a single point in space.

They have a beginning—but do they have an end? Ah! And here we have two differing viewpoints.

Geez! Can't they agree on anything?

Well, it's not that simple. And the theory you hold will influence a great deal, the rest of your thinking in this courtroom. So tread warily my friend and decide not hastily on the alternatives I set before you!

One school of thought believes that the hurtling galaxies will continue to travel in this expanding universe forever and ever. Since the volume and the surface area of the expanding balloon is continuously increasing and since no new material is being created anywhere in space, the density of the material will decrease until, finally, in infinite space, all of the matter and energy of the original explosion will be dissipated into virtual nothingness. The stars will burn all their fuel and the lights will die out one by one. The universe will have come to a dark, cold and silent end.

A beginning and an end!

The other school of thought—who do believe in the Big Bang—think that the galaxies, now traveling at enormous speeds, will slow down and eventually come to a halt. Gravitational forces between them will have applied the braking force. Then, slowly, they will start to move inward, toward that same center from which they started, picking up speed as they travel backward, compressing as the balloon becomes smaller and smaller, finally compacting into that same tiny volume of an apple, with incredible pressures building up within—to set off another cataclysmic explosion that sets matter and energy back into motion in a renewed cycle. An endless and infinite series of expansions and contractions. For all infinite time.

We are at present in the expansion cycle of such an explosion. But if this theory is correct, and since this current explosion is only one in an infinite series of such expansions and contractions—there has been no beginning either.

No beginning and no end!

But before you ask me to decide—and I know you will, because I'm beginning to know you better—let me ask. Is there any proof of the Big Bang theory itself?

Yes, there is. If you had an explosion, would you not have a thunder clap that would reverberate, dying down gradually with the passage of time?

Yes, there would.

So a primeval explosion of that intensity must have generated an enormously powerful outburst—not of sound, which cannot travel in a vacuum—but of radiation, which must fill all space and not be associated with any particular celestial body.

In 1965, two Bell Laboratory scientists, Arno Penzias and Robert Wilson, discovered in very sensitive radio receivers, a persistent hissing radio signal. It did not arise out of the radio system, could not be eliminated, and was not dependant on the direction in which the radio antenna was pointing.

They had discovered the faint remnants of the radiation that originated at the time of the Big Bang.

The proof is pretty conclusive that the universe originated in a single instant of creation. One moment it was not there, and the next it was! It is not I who say so. It is this physicist and astronomer who is giving the evidence and who says so. And now he is arguing with himself—unable to accept the conclusions of his own statements! He stated that if there is sufficient matter in the universe, the galaxies will come to a stop, recede backward to the same point that they started their journey from, and implode into it. The universe is a "closed universe". If there is not sufficient matter in the universe to slow down the galaxies, the universe will expand forever and ever, into limitless time. It is then an "open universe".

So which is it to be? What do his experiments reveal? Do his calculations tell us that there is sufficient matter, or there is not? It is a simple enough question!

And the answer, reluctantly given, is that there is not! There is not sufficient matter in the universe to slow down the galaxies.

We have an "open universe" that had one beginning and will have one end.

This conclusion does not please the physicists at all! They would prefer a closed universe, with infinite cycles of expansion and contraction, without beginning and without end. And the reason they prefer such a solution is because it does not permit us to ask the one question—which we will now ask—for which they have no answers!

What existed before the Big Bang? Why did the Big Bang take place? How did it take place? One beginning? So what was the state of affairs before it took place? What they would like to do is to avoid the crucial question of creation itself! They are able to bypass our question if they have a "closed universe"—but not if they have an "open universe"! So the search is on for more matter in the universe. How they would love to bypass the question of creation itself!

But we, the common people, will go only by the evidence that they themselves have presented to us in this courtroom. And that is that there is not sufficient matter in this universe for it to be a 'closed' one.

It is an "open universe", with one beginning and one end.

So we will ask the questions again.

What existed before the Big Bang?

Why did it take place at all?

How did it take place?

When it did take place, why did it take place in the precise manner in which it did?

Surely there must have been alternative ways in which the laws of physics could have been framed? Why does matter attract each other instead of repelling it? Or being indifferent to it? Why doesn't heat contract and cold expand?

See what I mean? Shall I go on and on?

Why have all the immutable laws of physics—and their exceptions—been framed in this precise way and no other? Where did all this energy come from? The energy in all those elementary particles that have now cooled and collected together to form the millions of galaxies with their trillions of stars—and all of the interstellar matter between!

And then again, why only just so many galaxies and not three more? Or three billion more? In a finite universe—and it is finite—the total energy content has to be finite too. A fixed quantity! No more or less; just right! Well, how was that decided and who decided that? May I know?

Stop! Stop! Please, stop! No more questions of this physicist. The poor man is in tears! He asks to be excused—at least for today. He will be back to answer our questions—your questions—if need be, but on some other day. Please? For my sake, will you let him go?

Very well. I didn't know you had a soft side to you! I thought I had him on the ropes and was just about ready to demolish him—were it not for your gracious intervention on his behalf.

Thank you. Now, you did say we would go by the evidence, did you not?

Yes, I did.

And that all the evidence would be permitted in this court?

Yes.

Then why have you not considered what the Bible says about the act of creation? Surely they, too, have a story to tell!

In the beginning God created the heavens and the earth. Now the earth was formless and empty, darkness was over the surface of the deep, and the Spirit of God was hovering over the waters.

And God said, "Let there be light," and there was light. God saw that the light was good, and he separated the light from the darkness. God called the light 'day' and the darkness he called 'night'. And there was evening, and there was morning—the first day.

And God said, "Let there be an expanse between the waters to separate water from water." So God made the expanse and separated the water under the expanse from the water above it. And it was so. God called the expanse 'sky'. And there was evening and there was morning—the second day.

Yet it was not until the fourth day that the stars were created.

And God said, "Let there be lights in the expanse of the sky to separate the day from the night, and let them serve as signs to mark seasons and days and years, and let there be lights in the expanse of the sky to give light on earth." And it was so. God made two great lights—the greater light to govern the day and the lesser light to govern the night. He also made the stars. God set them in the expanse of the sky to give light on the earth, to govern the day and the night, and to separate light from darkness. And God saw it was good. And there was evening and there was morning—the fourth day.

What did he create on the third day?

He made dry ground and the seas. And on the land he produced vegetation. Plants bearing seed according to their kind, and trees bearing fruit with seed in it according to their kinds.

The Bible is a book of revelation. Most religious beliefs are. That is their strength—and their weakness. As a revealed truth, it does not try to attempt scientific validation or experimental verification. It is above that. At times, it even disdains, the laws of logic. That is its strength! Its weakness lies in its inability to convince, even people of goodwill, that it is the absolute truth.

In approaching any book of revelation, there are two extremes, with several shades of middle ground in between.

One can approach such a work with total reverence. Every single word, every minute and inconsequential detail, is upheld as the absolute truth. To suggest otherwise is blasphemy! Hell and damnation await those who disagree, and retribution is at hand.

They are the lucky ones—those who keep such faith in the written word.

The other extreme is to find inconsequential details to be inconsistent with scientific truths and discard the entire work as being the figment of someone's fertile imagination. If the scientific method cannot be applied, the whole document has to be false! Since the Bible says that God made vegetation on the third day—a full day before he put the stars in the heavens—it is in conflict with scientific truth and becomes untenable!

Perhaps, such people don't look hard enough for the truth in anything.

A middle ground is to suggest that religious beliefs and the written word should be examined, not in the context of detailed accuracy but in the context of their impact upon us. We do not use the written word to prove or disprove anything; we use them to trace the way in which some very wise people, living in an age that had neither mathematics nor telescopes, used only their own intelligence and their view of the world around them—the evidence as they saw it—to try and explain precisely what we are attempting to do.

The nature of God! Can we fault them for that?

We are adjourned.

3

Zero Volume at Absolute Zero Temperature: Cause and Effect

I am sitting at the small table on the pavement of the roadside café—our courtroom—awaiting your arrival. But will you come? Perhaps, you no longer have an interest in these proceedings? Perhaps, you are upset at the way in which I cross—examined the last witness? Perhaps, you are quite right. I should have been more sympathetic to his confusion.

I look up and down the street. No sign of you. But then I came early—I always do—and you may still be on time or, perhaps, only a few minutes late.

Perhaps, you are interested in the subject, but you've been turned off by me! Personally, that is. I am not what you might have expected for a delightful day at a roadside café, sipping a glass of wine and discussing the mysteries of the universe.

Well, I'm sorry for that, but there's absolutely nothing I can do about it.

It is now almost the hour of our appointment. Still no sign of you in the street.

I feel your hand on my shoulder as you emerge from the café behind me and slide into the seat alongside of me.

I bought us two doughnuts. I trust you like to eat doughnuts?

Love them! And thank you for coming.

Thank me? I've had one of the most fascinating days of my life, sitting here beside you, sipping this delicious wine, and listening to the evidence. I could never have stayed away! Besides you do need me, you know. To maintain a sense of balance to the arguments you advance; to prevent you from being obsessed with your own pre-conceived ideas. Not looking at the facts with that objectivity of the impersonal observer!

Yes, I do need you. If for no other reason than for us to talk. Bouncing all that evidence we are receiving off two minds is better than bouncing it off one. Shall we begin?

What existed before the Big Bang?

Physicists and astronomers refuse to answer the question.

Physicists say that they are concerned with a study of the laws of physics. Before the Big Bang, the laws of physics, presumably, did not exist! So such a question falls outside the purview of their deliberations.

Astronomers hide behind the physicists. If physics cannot predict theories before the Big Bang, what precisely are we looking for with our telescopes? Besides, if there was no light and no radiation and no emissions before the Big Bang, what will we see with our telescopes anyway?

But we are neither physicists nor astronomers. We can ask the question, and with a little bit of logic and a lot of hard, truthful thinking, we can even begin to answer it.

But, first, we have to understand another set of very simple laws that govern the behaviour of gases. They are called the Gas Laws.

The first of these simple laws is Boyle's Law. Robert Boyle, an Anglo-Irish physicist and chemist, the seventh son of the First Earl of Cork, was born in 1627. In 1662, at the age of 35, he invented a vacuum pump to study the behaviour of gases, and came to the conclusion that if he compressed the gas into a small volume, the pressure increased. When he expanded the gas into a larger volume, sure enough, the pressure decreased. So he made the simple statement that the pressure and the volume of the gas were in inverse proportion to one another. The higher the pressure the smaller the volume; the smaller the pressure, the larger the volume.

So if the volume of the gas is zero, the pressure must be infinite! This was all very theoretical, of course. It had to be a perfect gas. In any case, it was impossible to reduce the volume of the gas to nothingness, because the pressure would be infinite and the pump would promptly explode!

J.A.C. Charles was a French physicist, born in 1746. He dabbled in many things such as confirming the electrical experiments of Benjamin Franklin, and ascending to a height of almost two miles using a balloon filled with hydrogen gas.

He, too, stated a very simple law governing the behaviour of perfect gases. He said that the volume was proportional to the temperature of the gas. Reduce the temperature and you reduce the volume. Gay—Lussac, also a French physicist and chemist, showed, in 1802 that in fact this contraction of volume with a fall in temperature was the same for all gases. Even that seemed simple enough, until an examination of various gases showed that, strangely enough for all gases, the lines of contracting volumes all converged to zero volume at the same temperature!

A temperature of –273.15°C. At that temperature, the gas existed, but did not occupy a volume.

It disappeared into nothingness!

In the laboratories of the world, for low—temperature physics, the frantic hunt was on to reach the temperature of –273.15°C—or Absolute Zero. We have reached within a few millionths of a degree of this temperature, but we cannot actually ever reach it. The theory tells us that for all matter—whether on Earth or in the universe, even in empty space itself—the temperature cannot fall to –273.15°C or below. If it did, a perfect gas would disappear, as it occupies zero volume.

It contracts into nothingness!

It seems a simple enough temperature. –273.15°C. We are not talking about a thousand degrees or a million degrees below the freezing point of water! Just –273.15°C. And yet, at the upper end of the scale, it is possible to hit temperatures as hot as 10 billion degrees, because that is the estimated temperature at the time of the Big Bang. Even our own Sun, which is really a small star compared to many in the universe, has a temperature at the core of about 20 million degrees.

What is so interesting about Absolute Zero is that it forms an absolute limit in our existence. Physicists do not say that, with more sophisticated equipment, they will reach it one day! On the contrary, their own theory tells them that it can never be reached in any finite length of time! It is a line we may never touch; a line we may never cross.

So we ask the question. What exists on the other side of the line? What would be the state of the universe on the other side of the line? It is a simple enough question.

The temperature must be –273.15°C. We have already established that. All of the energy, at that temperature, would occupy zero volume—at infinite pressures. Space would be empty, but since space itself is nothingness, and occupies no volume, it is the only rational quantity that can exist at that temperature.

But does space itself exist?

It is a question that deals with the relative nature of the objects in it. We can conceive of space only when we think about objects within that space. By thinking about the distance between the objects, we define the quantity that enables us to perceive it. Remove all objects in space—every single one—and space too disappears! Particularly when we remove the envelope, or the outer boundaries that we perceive as enclosing space.

An unenclosed space, without any objects in it and so without a frame of reference, is nothingness!

So too with time.

Time is the interval between events. As long as there is even one single event taking place—in the entire universe, anywhere—time exists, if not for us then for an observer in space. But if you were to bring every single event, in the entire universe, to a halt, then time too, like space, disappears!

And there we have it. The state of affairs that existed before the Big Bang. A temperature of –273.15°C—and a nothingness, contained within a nothingness, in a timelessness. Now if no energy existed at that time, then there were no conditions for the explosive nature of the Big Bang. But if energy did exist in a zero volume on the other side of the line, then it was contained at infinite, but stable, pressures.

How much energy?

Whatever is the sum total of the energy in the universe. And it is finite. There we have it. All of it was contained on the other side of the line, prevented from coming into being by a temperature of Absolute Zero, or –273.15°C.

But what we also do know is that, as of now, the universe is on this side of Absolute Zero—and has been so for several billion years. So at some time, the temperature of all that energy must have arisen by an infinitesimally small value above Absolute Zero. And here we pause to ask ourselves a series of questions that we must answer first before we can proceed. These are rather nice doughnuts!

Thank you. I think so too.

Tomorrow, it will be my turn to provide them. That's fair.

Okay. But, please, where have we reached? Where is the universe—on the other side of the line or on our side of the line?

It is still on the other side. But before we bring it over onto this side of the line we have to try and answer five questions. Or at least some of them!

How? Who? What with? When? Why?

The 'How' is easy to understand. By raising the temperature of all that energy that is our universe by a fraction of a degree past Absolute Zero. In fractions of a second—it is estimated at one millionth of it—all that energy suddenly came into being and occupied a volume. Nothingness became something, all at the same point, and the resulting explosion could only have been cataclysmic. And because there was now an 'object' in it, space, too, came into being. The temperature rocketed from –273.15°C to a temperature of ten billion degrees. Oh! What a sight it must have been!

We know that the millions of galaxies, with their trillions of stars and all of the interstellar matter between, all arose out of the Big Bang, and the finite amount of 'matter' that was then contained as energy in that explosion may even be calculated. As you can imagine, it is an incredibly large quantity—but it is still finite.

Within a few thousandth of a second, all of that energy was in the form of elementary particles, some so exotic they died right there or were converted into other particles. We may never know what they were because we cannot recreate—in a laboratory—the conditions of the Big Bang. From one hundredth of a second to about 100 seconds after the Big Bang, the universe consisted of photons, electrons, positrons, neutrinos, antineutrinos, protons, neutrons—add a few more—if you wish! Energy was well on its way to becoming matter, with the temperatures now steadily dropping as the elementary particles and the radiation rocketed away. And as they did, they created their own envelope of space. Space was being expanded!

It would be very easy for us to proceed, hastily, from that scenario to the present day. But there is still one unanswered questions we must first resolve before we can leave that event of creation.

Did the Laws of Physics exist before the Big Bang or were they, as some suggest, formulated during the Big Bang? Before we attempt to answer that question, it would be just as well to lay down the ground rules of logic that will permeate our thinking and force us to reach conclusions that are not acceptable to us—even appear to be absurd! What then do we do? Accept the logic and the absurdity—or refuse to accept both?

Let us say that we see a black dog walking down the street.

Is it on a leash? I'm nervous around ownerless dogs that are not on a leash.

Relax! The dog is on a leash and the pretty owner is not far behind. May I proceed?

Please do.

We cannot make the generalisation that all dogs are black. That would be unacceptable because our experience has produced dogs that are white and brown and red and many shades in between. However, can we reach the conclusion that all dogs have four legs—even the ones we haven't seen? I think we can. Our experience clearly seems to indicate that it is so, even though we have no 'proof' of it. We may well discover a one-legged, two-legged, or three—legged normal, non—amputated dog around the corner, but in the absence of that discovery we are permitted the conclusion that all dogs have four legs. Is that fair?

Yes.

However, we cannot reach the conclusion that every four-legged animal is a dog, because our experience clearly shows us cows and elephants that have four legs and are not dogs.

Did the Laws of Physics exist before the Big Bang?

We can not speak for all the Laws of Physics, but we can say that at least one law did exist before the Big Bang—the gas law that held all that energy—

filled universe in zero volume at a temperature of Absolute Zero, and then brought it into being with the fractional rise in temperature above –273.15ºC.

One law of physics, that exists with us today, that can be proved by theory though never tested in a laboratory, that is both immutable and inviolate, did exist before the Big Bang, and therefore had to have been decreed as a Law before the Big Bang.

May we make the assumption that all the Laws of Physics, which are immutable and inviolate, were, therefore, also in place and decreed as Laws before the Big Bang?

I think we can.

Good! But, by definition, a 'Law' has to be 'made' or 'put into place'. That implies that there must be a 'Law Maker' who made the law and put it into place, must it not?

Yes. God?

If you want to call him that.

What would you like to call him? Are you afraid to use the word?

Yes, I am hesitant to use the word because the word 'God' immediately conjures up images of an all-powerful, all-seeing, all-knowing, being—and we do not really have the evidence to affirm that at this time.

He could certainly raise the temperature of a finite energy level above Absolute Zero by fractions of a degree, and he certainly knows his physics—but we cannot jump to the conclusion that he knows how to sing!

I see the problem. You don't want to generalise.

At least not until all the evidence is in. Some scientists prefer to think of a 'Directed Intelligence'. The word is not mine. It has been in usage for a while now. May I suggest a compromise?

I'm listening.

We will call this Directed Intelligence 'God'. For one thing it is a nice short word! But we will not have any preconceived notions of what we mean by it. We will not ascribe to it any qualities—at least not until we have specific evidence of a particular quality that he possesses, after which we will assume, in all future discussion that he does indeed possess that quality. Notice that I have used the word 'qualities' and not 'properties'. And yet, we may really be meaning just that. Not qualities but properties! We cannot think of him as being an individual, simply because he may not be one. Perhaps, he has some of the properties we would normally associate with inanimate objects and some of the properties we would ascribe to people. Or both!

I notice that you are not capitalising the 'h' when you refer to him.

I have no wish to embarrass him. Does that seem like a reasonable approach? We will use the word 'God' not quite fully knowing what we mean, defining him better in time, based on the evidence as it comes in.

What precisely do we know of him, as of now, may I ask?

Certainly. He initiated the moment of creation. He formulated and put in place the laws of physics that would govern the universe.

What with? Where did he get all that energy from—the energy that would form the universe? Did he 'create' it?

Difficult question!

It is. Because if he 'created' it then we have to ask how, and from what, did he create the energy that was to form the universe? What existed before he created it? Can he create something that did not exist in some form?

So we come to the inescapable conclusion that the energy that he used—was himself. He is the only entity that we know existed before the Big Bang. He had to have existed to put into place the laws of physics that he formulated. We have no evidence of anything else. And we did say we would go only by the evidence! Some may well argue that he, being God, had the capability to create anything in any quantity and at any time, but that logic is ascribing to him powers he may not possess—or at least, powers we have not proven him to possess!

So—as of now—we have to reach the logical conclusion that he used his own 'energy' to form the universe. And what a magnificent store of energy! All those millions of galaxies and their trillions of stars, with planets and moons and comets, and interstellar matter between them—all of it is quite simply the body of God. Every pebble on the beach, every drop of water in the oceans, every cloud in the sky, is him. Every doorknob, or brick, or skyscraper is built out of him. Everything—quite simply—is him!

I get the picture. Let us go to When? Before you turn all poetic on me!

When did he create the universe? The scientists are more forthcoming on that evidence. About ten to thirteen billion years ago. That is the estimated time from the Big Bang. So we come to the last question.

Why?

That question we will have to leave for a very long time—until all the evidence is in. But we can start—with the evidence that is in—to ascribe to him other knowledge that he must undoubtedly possess. We have already ascribed him one—a knowledge of physics.

I'm loving this!

With the evidence, we can safely assume that he knew about 'cause' and 'effect'.

Beg your pardon?

Science tells us that, in all of its branches—physics, chemistry, biology, you name it—without exception, every cause has an effect. A specific cause has a specific effect. In quantitative terms, for a given amount of cause there is a precisely defined amount of effect—always! It is also, strangely, a one—way street. The effect may certainly be the cause for some other effect, but it can never be the cause for the first cause.

Please! Please! You are losing me! Give me an example.

Certainly. Imagine you are holding two flint stones in your hand. When you strike them you will produce a spark will you not?

Yes. Very likely. If I strike them hard enough. Maybe not at the first attempt. Yes, I will produce a spark.

Well, the striking of the two flint stones together is the cause; the spark is the effect, wouldn't you say?

Yes. And I presume that there is a law of physics that governs it?

Precisely! Now the spark can never be the cause of your striking the two flint stones together. So it is a one-way street. The spark could well be the cause of starting a fire in the forest, but the fire is not the cause of the spark. The fire could well be the cause of an animal dying in the forest, but the death of the animal is not the cause of the fire. This example relates to our common experience, but, in science, it is possible to define in mathematical terms, equations that express such cause and effect in quantitative terms, so that both cause and effect are more precisely defined. And it is always a one-way street!

This does not mean that actions are not reversible. Not at all. So many are, but each has its own set of cause and effect. For instance, the right amount of hydrogen and the right amount of oxygen will give us a precise quantity of water. Cause and effect. The water may then be split up into its constituent hydrogen and oxygen elements, but that is a separate reaction with its own cause and effect. We will get a lot more evidence on cause and effect from other disciplines, but even his very first action permits us to make a statement about the nature of God.

He must have known about cause and effect!

The raising of the temperature of all that energy, that was to form the universe, by a fraction of a degree above Absolute Zero, was the cause. The Big Bang was the effect. Knowledge of the Laws of Physics, that he had himself formulated, must imply his knowledge of all the effect that his actions would have on the still unborn universe. And, since, in science, precise causes have precise effects which can be mathematically calculated, it implies that he was fully aware and knowledgeable of all the effects of the laws that he had put into place, must it not? They are not random laws, that act at some time and not at others! An unopposed force acting on a body causes it to move. Cause and effect. Here, on Earth and in the Andromeda galaxy! Heat expands and cold contracts. Cause and effect. Here on Earth and in some black hole! It is a scientifically ordered universe, by all accounts. May we assume that he knew about cause and effect?

I think we can. I think we must. To assume otherwise is to imply that the Maker of the Laws did not appreciate their significance or the effects they would have while compelling the universe to obey those same laws! And if indeed, creation was an act of capriciousness, with total disregard for the effects of his own laws, we would see a chaotic and disorderly physical universe around us—which we do not!

By decreeing a state of affairs that was inexorably dependant on cause and effect, he has ensured a rigid obedience to his laws. And, with the evidence before us, we can now, with confidence, ascribe to God one very simple quality that he possessed.

Knowledge.

4

Knowledge

Knowledge. How do we define it?

A simple dictionary definition reads as follows:

"A result or product of knowing; information or understanding acquired through experience, practical ability or skill. Deep and extensive learning; erudition. The cumulative culture of the human race. A sure conviction; certainty. The act, process or state of knowing; cognition. Any object of knowing or mental apprehension; that which is or may be known. Specific information; notice. Archaic: Sexual intercourse: often preceded by carnal."

And there we have it. All the ways in which we may think of 'knowledge'. Setting aside the archaic, as not quite what we had in mind, all of the other definitions merely illustrate the various ways in which the word 'knowledge' may be used in the English language.

We will, however, need to probe deeper than the dictionary definitions to establish the real meaning of knowledge. And, when in doubt, we will fall back on our 'label' as 'common people' to ask all the right questions!

What may be known?

How may it be known?

Who may know?

And the very nice thing about it is that, though we think these are tough questions, by arguing it between us, you and I, we may find the answers as well.

The first question is the easiest to answer. What may be known?

Everything. Anything and everything at all, whether in the realm of human experience or outside it, whether capable of being proved or not, anything that may be imagined or is unimaginable by us—all this constitutes knowledge. The way birds fly, that two plus two is four, the origins of the universe, extra sensory perception, good grammar, bad grammar, how to brew good coffee—all this and much, much more constitute knowledge.

Does bad grammar constitute knowledge too?

Oh, yes! The fact that it can be acquired by some—much to the distress of others—is proof that it constitutes knowledge. Undesirable knowledge, for sure, but knowledge nevertheless. What distinguishes knowledge from every other abstract concept is that it is totally and completely independent of everything else—even God himself! Space needs objects within it to exist, and time needs a succession of events in order to pass, but knowledge has always existed and will always continue to exist, regardless of the existence or otherwise of any other entity. Abstract knowledge can exist even in the absence of God.

Come now! Isn't that going a bit too far? After all without God there would have been no universe and so no knowledge.

Wrong! Even without God, or the Big Bang, or the universe, knowledge—all of it—has always existed. In fact we say: 'God had knowledge'. Let me put it another way. The knowledge of the way in which a motor car works existed long before there was a motor car or gasoline or the science of thermodynamics! Knowledge can only be discovered. It cannot be invented. Discovery implies pre-existence, does it not?

True.

And so every piece of knowledge, whether useful or not, whether discovered by us now, or to be discovered by us in the future, or never, ever to be discovered by us, on every aspect of everything—already exists! What we do know is that we are not aware of some of that knowledge, but it would be a sad day if we were to deny the existence of all that of which we are not aware!

So all knowledge exists as of right now?

Precisely! When we discover a piece of knowledge, we acquire it. Consider the simple statement that two plus two equals four. You and I had to learn it at school. And billions of other children learn it as well. Yet, were the human race to be wiped off the face of the Earth, the fact that two plus two equals four still continues to be around. The Earth may well be ruled by rodents who are unaware of it, but many millions of years later, with a growth in their brain capacity, they, too, might well discover that two plus two equals four!

Knowledge does not need anything else to exist as an abstract concept, not even its appreciation or discovery. Because that is precisely what it is—a non-physical, abstract concept.

The second question—how it may be known—is a lot more difficult to answer.

But we're going to try anyway.

You begin to know me better and better! Yes, we're going to try anyway. It is easy to see that at least some of the knowledge we acquire reaches us through the senses—sight, hearing, smell, touch and taste. They are far from perfect. In us, they are not particularly well-developed. Dogs have better sense of smell than we have. The bloodhound would put us to shame! Bats use radar to fly. Migratory birds, working through their senses, can navigate for thousands of miles with uncanny accuracy! The lowly scallop has eyes set round the edge of the shell so that it has 360 vision. Insects have antennae to extend their sense of touch. It is only, perhaps, in the sense of taste that we come out on top in the Animal Kingdom. The vast range of culinary delights of people, from all over the world, convinces me of that. Anybody who enjoys good food has much to be grateful for being born human!

The sensory receptors merely receive stimuli and transmit them to the brain. There, in the cortex, the ultimate analysis of the sensory data takes place, and the information is then fed to other parts of the brain, to induce muscle movement, or to store in the memory or, perhaps, to discard. It is in all of these brain functions, with the ten billion or so interconnected brain cells and the innumerable pathways that they provide, that the human brain is peerless! And located within the corpus callosum are the seats of reasoning, learning, and, perhaps, the memory search.

It is a far from perfect way to acquire knowledge. Imagine that you and I are standing, on a cloudless night, looking up at a star. The light from that star may have started out three billion years ago—if the star is three billion year light years away from us. When it reaches us, on this night, we are looking at it as it was three billion years ago. Not today! Today we don't know what it looks like and whether it even exists! What is happening on that star today will not be known to us for another three billion years.

And even if we are content to know what it looked like three billion years ago, we still have cause for great dissatisfaction. All we see with the naked eye is a pinpoint of light. Were we to look at it through a small telescope we would see it better, and were we to look at it through a larger telescope we would see it even better. So the knowledge of that star is based on far from perfect receiving devices—and is out of date by only three billion years!

Our senses will always be limited. And the information we receive through them, which is then processed by the brain into knowledge, will, therefore, be always limited and incomplete. It is as if in the very act of 'knowing' we blur knowledge and smear it—to which we then proceed to apply reasoning and logical deductions to form conclusions. Change the senses and we would change our perceptions of the physical world around us.

Imagine that the light from a nearby object in an open field reaches my eye and I perceive it to be a tree. Everyone I ask assures me that I am correct, because they, too, perceive it to be a tree. When I describe what I see to them they confirm that that is precisely what they see. Until I ask an alien, with a different eye structure, what is it that he sees, and he gives me a totally different description of the object. Perhaps his eyes can see only the atomic structure of the object, and all he can see are the atoms, with their protons and neutrons forming the core, and the electrons spinning in shells around them! Certainly matter when looked at through an electron microscope is quite different from what we may see with the naked eye.

What the alien and I would be able to agree upon is that there is an object out there in the field that is sending us a stimulus. The both of us perceive the stimulus differently, and reach widely differing views on the nature of that object. Neither of us will deny the stimulus!

The reality may never be known! The act of knowing imposes on that reality an image—which is all we can 'know'.

Fortunately for us, that restriction applies only to the knowledge we gain through our senses. It does not apply to the abstract knowledge we acquire through the process of reasoning and deduction. For instance, both the alien and I, regardless of our senses, would be able to agree that, in fact, there is an object out there that is sending us the stimulus. Because by the process of reasoning and deduction, both he and I arrive at the same conclusion.

But reasoning, such a powerful tool of the human mind, can lead to erroneous conclusions, if the original premise or assumption on which the reasoning is based is itself in error. For instance, suppose I were to make the statement that two plus two is not four, but is equal to three! This is an erroneous assumption. I now apply to it the reasoning that if I double both sides of the equal—to sign, they will still be equal. And so I have eight equals six! If I apply the reasoning that if I triple both sides of the equal—to sign, they will still be equal.

I arrive at the conclusion that twelve equals nine! The reasoning that I have used is perfectly correct, but the answers are still very wrong because the original premise was in error.

Reasoning, by itself, may not always lead to correct conclusions.

We are discussing the ways in which knowledge may be acquired. In the human condition, the senses together with reasoning do just that for us. But knowledge can be acquired in more ways than that.

Consider animals. They acquire knowledge through instinct. Food gathering, reproductive procedures and the nest—building drives of birds are all examples of knowledge that is acquired at birth by being indelibly printed in the genetic code. There appears to be no conscious, thought—induced mental process that would involve even the most rudimentary use of intelligence.

The animal just knows!

Can you accept that? That knowledge may be acquired without the use of intelligence?

Yes. But the creature is unaware that it has that knowledge.

Possibly. We won't argue that one. But consider the genetic code that contains hereditary information to be transmitted from one generation to the next. The genes, passed on to the new born baby, contain information on the colour of his eyes and hair, the shape of his nose, the type of bone structure he will inherit, even the diseases that he will be susceptible to! If it is a girl, in addition to all these and many more, the genetic code will determine her chances of successful motherhood! Is this not a transfer of 'knowledge' from one generation to the next?

Yes, I would say so.

And the acquisition of that knowledge had nothing to do with intelligence at all. The transfer of that knowledge has nothing to do with intelligence either. What we have here is knowledge contained in the genes—as a form of biological memory. And so I will now ask you straight out.

Do you agree with me that genes have 'knowledge'?

Yes.

But they are not aware of it.

No. It is a form of biological 'memory'.

But it is knowledge! It was acquired. It is stored. It is used. I think it passes every test that may be applied to what constitutes the acquisition of knowledge. So we may then go one step further. Do inanimate objects also store knowledge and act on it without being aware of it?

You mean stones?

If you drop a stone from a tower it falls to the ground. The force of gravity causes it to accelerate towards the earth. Now, one may say that it is law of physics—and it is—but one could ask the question as to how the laws of physics demand and obtain compliance from inanimate objects? I think the answer is that compliance to the laws of physics is obtained from inanimate objects by having the laws intrinsic to the material itself! Just as the genetic code has a biological 'memory', so too inanimate objects have an imprinted compliance to physical laws—a sort of obedience—without which the material could not even exist!

But that too is 'knowledge'. Acquired by the material as a condition to its existence! Used by it without awareness, as a natural response—just like the nest—building drives of birds, or the instinctive response of a seed of grass to earth and water. That knowledge, contained in a law that is fundamental to the behaviour of the material, lies at one end of the spectrum; reasoning to extend knowledge, lies at the other—with all of the various shades of instinct in between.

Which has answered the third of our questions. Who may know?

Everything may 'know'. It is how we define the act of 'knowing' or what we may 'know' that is different. So on that definition, would you be comfortable with my saying that God had all knowledge of every conceivable kind! Knowledge of the laws of physics, the nest—building drives of birds, good grammar, bad grammar, two plus two equals four, how a motor car works, differential equations in higher mathematics—you can name it and he knew all about it.

Why do you keep saying that he 'had' it? Or that he 'knew' all about it? In the past tense! Does he not have it now?

The only evidence that has been placed before us—as of now—has been from the astronomer and the physicist. And that relates to the state of affairs at the time of the Big Bang. But thirteen billion years, or so, have passed since then. We will need to have more evidence placed before us in order to decide whether he still has all that knowledge. Or did he, voluntarily, choose to divest himself of some, or all, of it?

5

The Ability of Elementary Particles to Diversify into Matter

It is now 100 seconds after the Big Bang. The entire universe to be now consists of elementary particles—photons, electrons, protons, neutrons, neutrinos, and a few more we know nothing about and never will—myriads of them, all just born. Some have such short lives that they've just died. They were born and they died! But the laws of atomic physics, that deal with the behaviour of such elementary particles at sub-atomic level, have also been framed and so, presumably, each elementary particle 'knew' how to behave in precisely the way in which it was meant to behave.

Matter has no free will.

Do we?

Shall we leave that discussion for later? We're still only a 100 seconds past the Big Bang! Do you mind?

You're not trying to avoid the subject, now are you?

I promise we will come back to it. Word of honor!

Then let us proceed. What then?

The steadily dropping temperatures, with the rapidly expanding universe, brings other laws of physics into force to determine what will happen next. There was no uncertainty about it—whatever is uncertain is because we just don't know—but the elementary particles sure knew what they were supposed to do!

One such law, that we do know, said that the proton would be positively charged and the electron would be negatively charged, and they would attract each other.

There would be a chemistry between them! The proton would be considerably heavier than the electron, but with the electron travelling at such fantastic speeds, the proton could only 'capture' the electron in just the same way as the Earth has captured the moon. The electron would orbit the nucleus, that is the proton, that had captured it.

One electron orbiting one proton—and we have hydrogen. It was the first element to be formed. The very first! And to this day it is the simplest of all the elements. Its atomic structure is so simple; it has an atomic number of one. An atom of hydrogen has one proton and one electron. This is the most common form of hydrogen, called protium. But even in those first few seconds, laws had been initiated that would radically change the nature of the universe. If a single neutron—which has no charge—attached itself to the proton in the nucleus, the protium hydrogen was converted into an isotope called deuterium. This might not suggest anything of much significance, until we realise that the properties of protium and deuterium differ slightly!

Both physical and chemical properties of the atom had changed by the addition of a single neutron to the nucleus.

With the addition of another neutron, the hydrogen formed yet another isotope—tritium—with its properties slightly different from either of the other two.

But as yet, there was only one proton in the nucleus and one electron spinning around it. The addition of neutrons, to the nucleus, did not change the element—merely produced different varieties of it, some common and some very rare. But when two protons fused together, with their captured electrons of course, the material that resulted was helium.

And helium has properties that are radically different from hydrogen!

Hydrogen is the lightest of all gases. It is highly inflammable, forms over 75 per cent of the known universe and is the fuel for the stars, including our own sun. Helium on the other hand is the second lightest gas, is both inert and non-combustible and forms about 23 per cent of the universe. These radically different physical and chemical properties arose out of the very simple step of having two protons in the nucleus instead of just one.

Why? Why should the number of protons, with their satellite electrons, make so much difference to the physical and chemical properties of the element? There is no answer from the chemists—except to say that is the way it is! Let three protons form the nucleus and we have lithium. Let six of them form the nucleus and we have carbon.

Let eight protons decide to come together and form the nucleus—and we have oxygen. With an atomic number of eight. All these protons and electrons, whether they form the hydrogen atom or the carbon atom or the oxygen atom are all identical elementary particles. Yet the properties of the elements they produce are so different from each other.

Matter had found a way to diversify!

Before we jump to any conclusions from this truly extraordinary capability of the particles—and there are so many, very exciting ones we can reach—we ought to clarify the question of 'intent'.

Intent?

Yes. Whether there was intent or not?

I thought that was obvious! That there was intent. Knowledge of cause and effect. I thought that we'd discussed that at some length!

Not quite. Let me run a scenario by you, and you tell me what conclusions you draw. Agreed?

I'm listening to your story.

A lecture is being held in a small auditorium. The lights are on. The speaker has not as yet arrived. The audience is sparse. There are plenty of vacant seats in every row.

On the very first row, in a seat on the center aisle, a girl unbuttons her coat, brushes the hair back from her eyes, and looks at herself in her make-up mirror. She is satisfied with what she sees.

Pretty girl?

Very! Now, five minutes later, a young man walks down the center aisle from the entrance at the back, seeking a suitable place to seat himself—for what could be a long and boring lecture. He passes the six rows from the back, passes rows five, four and three, hesitates, passes row two, and reaches the first row.

The aisle seat is taken. There are twelve other vacant seats in the same row. He hesitates for a second; then sits down beside the pretty girl. Tell me, could you draw conclusions from watching his behaviour?

I most certainly could!

I'm listening.

You've clearly stated that she is a very pretty girl, is she not?

Yes.

There are so many vacant seats; yet he chooses to sit beside her?

Right again.

Well, then the only conclusion I can draw is that he is trying to pick her up!

I wouldn't be quite so quick to reach that conclusion. What you have concluded, from the facts that are undeniable, needs to be validated by 'intent'. In this case, the young man's 'intent' in sitting beside the pretty young girl. While you could be right, there is another possibility; quite simply that he knows her.

But you did say he hesitated coming down the rows; then hesitated again before he sat down beside her!

Yes, he did. The facts are undeniable. He was searching for her in the auditorium, and when a man is doing that, he will hesitate as he passes rows of seats with people in those rows, because his eyes are not fully coordinated with his feet—and he is looking at them from behind. A man, in a suit, will also hesitate for a moment to unbutton his jacket before he sits, to relieve the stress on the buttons.

That's not fair! Why didn't you tell me that he knows her?

Because we don't know that as a fact! Only her actions when he sits down beside her will decide that. If she gets up in a huff, crosses the aisle to a seat in the row on the other side down—avoiding his eyes though the anger in her own would be enough to set him on fire—then we could conclude that he was trying to pick her up and failed!

If, on the other hand, she takes his arm and cuddles up close to him, then we can conclude, with confidence, that they do know each other, and that he was searching her out in the auditorium.

Well, what did she do?

At that precise moment, there was a power failure in the auditorium, and I'm afraid we don't know. All the evidence is not in for us to reach a conclusion.

That's most unfair! You're telling the story! Why was it necessary to have a power failure at that precise instant of time?

To illustrate the point that in the absence of evidence, the question of 'intent' becomes very important—and very difficult to determine! The facts are clear, but what were the young man's intentions?

Are you going to tell me the end of this story or not? I hate enigmatic endings! I'll even bribe you with a second doughnut!

That is not necessary. When the lights came on, a few minutes later, the elderly couple in the second row are scandalised to see the young man and the pretty girl locked in a loving kiss! With an embarrassed smile, they apologise to the couple in the row behind, and settle down to the lecture. Her arm is in his, their thighs touch; she looks radiant. And when the lecture is over they go home.

His or hers?

Theirs. They've been married for seven years; two children. A boy and a girl. The most beautiful kids you ever saw—and so well—behaved. A real delight! Didn't I tell you? Must have slipped my mind.

You're a romantic. But you've made your point. No drawing of conclusions on 'intent' until all the evidence is in.

Precisely! It would be easy to say that because matter had found a way to diversify—and it had—that God intended it so be so. We can certainly say with full conviction that the laws of physics were framed in such a way that it was possible for matter to diversify; even that it was very likely that it would diversify! Here again we come up against the enormity of actions and interactions that were to occur after the Big Bang, and the possibility, or otherwise, of having knowledge of, and orchestrating, every single one of those actions and interactions between the elementary particles for reaching, with intent, some final result.

Did God know, or did he not know, what was going to happen? Did he want it, and so fully intend it to happen, or it did not concern him?

You have summarised my concerns beautifully. He had all knowledge, knew about cause and effect, framed the laws of atomic physics, and so was fully knowledgeable about the actions his laws would have on the elementary particles—how could he have not known that matter would diversify? And since the laws were framed so that matter would diversify, we have to reach the inescapable conclusion that he fully intended it to diversify!

But does that imply that he knew about every single interaction between every proton and every electron—and there are trillions upon trillions upon trillions of such interactions! One vast, cosmic computer that keeps tabs on all of them—and everything?

Is there?

Let me postpone the question by running another little scenario by you.

Oh, no! Not again! I'm listening, though.

Two high school teams are playing a soccer match. One of the boys has a heart defect of which he is unaware. As a result of the physical exercise, after the match, he collapses on the field. An ambulance is called to rush him to the hospital. On the way to the hospital, with its sirens blazing and lights flashing, the ambulance has an accident with a car, and a young woman in the car dies.

Oh, dear!

Sad, I agree, but in writing this story it was necessary that the young woman die. Now tell me, what are the essential events that must be in place for the young woman to die? The boys must be playing soccer. The boy must have a heart defect. He must have physical exercise for his heart to collapse. The ambulance must have the accident. Would you agree?

Yes.

So it is not necessary for us—writing the story—to know, or even care about, how many shots were taken at the goal by either side, how many times any particular boy had the ball passed to him, how many times the soccer ball was out of bounds, what was the final score, or whatever! Was there?

Just so long as matter diversified, it was not necessary to know the individual movement of every individual proton or electron or neutron—knowing that in that maelstrom interaction between the elementary particles would take place—and matter would surely diversify!

One does not need a vast, cosmic computer to predict it!

We are not drawing conclusions—merely receiving evidence from the chemists. Atoms combined to form molecules. A molecule is the smallest part of a substance that exhibits the properties and nature of that substance. Divide a molecule and you do not have that substance. A molecule of hydrogen is very small. It consists of only two atoms connected together by a chemical bond between them. This chemical bond is not anywhere as strong as the physical bond between the proton and the electron. The chemical bond can be easily broken in a chemical reaction, permitting single atoms of one substance to connect with atoms of another substance, to form complex compounds.

An example is water. If two atoms of hydrogen combine with one atom of oxygen, the resulting molecule is water. It is written as H_2O. If one atom of carbon combines with two atoms of oxygen, we have carbon dioxide, written as CO_2.

Matter can continue to diversify. But we had better cut short the testimony of this chemist who is giving evidence before us—or he will try to teach us all of chemistry! Perhaps he is a university professor who has written a textbook on the subject?

I agree completely. That is not the purpose of this inquiry—to learn chemistry or every other discipline. His evidence has been valuable. The facts are undeniable.

The Big Bang need not have produced elementary particles—but it did.

A proton need not have been born positively charged and an electron need not have been born with a negative charge—but they were—leading to hydrogen atoms.

All intercourse between hydrogen atoms could have ceased, leaving the entire universe filled with hydrogen and nothing else—but it didn't. The atoms, colliding together, fused their nuclei into atoms that were heavier than hydrogen, and the chain had commenced—into heavier elements like carbon and oxygen, and then in the interiors of stars and in the vastness of space into diversified matter.

I think, more than the origin of life, this constitutes the real start of evolution and the journey to where we are today. Because a principle had been put into place—matter could diversify! It was the start of a very long road to the formation of some of the most complex molecules—the amino acids.

Was there intent?

I think there was. There is no element of 'chance' in all of the evidence that we have received up to this point. Neither physicist, nor astronomer nor chemist has suggested, even vaguely, that any of the laws that started us on this journey are random laws. The laws are too specific for them to be random. Neither are they randomly applied. Not here on Earth, nor on Mars nor in the Andromeda galaxy.

They are too specific for them to operate and control matter, as they do, without it being fully intentional.

There was intent.

6

The Evidence of the Biochemist

Who shall we invite today? To sit at our table and give evidence before us.

Why, the biochemist, of course.

She wants to tell us about all the wondrous events taking place in the hydrosphere above the Earth. About four billion years ago—give or take half a billion—the lithospheric crust of the Earth had begun to form. But the extremely hot temperatures on the surface of the Earth would not permit any liquid with a low boiling point—least of all water—to stay on it. The result was that all of the water, formed by the combination of hydrogen and oxygen atoms, was held in the atmosphere as water vapor in a huge, thick, hollow sphere that girdled the earth at a safe distance from it; unable to leave it because of the gravitational forces and unable to descend to it because of the heat! Within that hydrosphere, in addition to all the water that was to descend to the surface of the Earth and eventually form the oceans, there were other basic elements of simple types such as carbon and nitrogen.

In order to understand the origins of life on earth—and that is what she is leading up to—we have to visualise the conditions that prevailed at that time. The surface of the Earth was wrinkled and contorted, with active volcanoes and open fissures reaching deep down into the molten interior. The fissures gushed forth even more exotic elements that ran like rivers on the sizzling surface, and the volcanoes erupted with unimaginable ferocity to hurl some of these heavier elements, as ash and lava, into the hydrosphere. The water vapor condensed to form rain, touched the surface of the boiling earth and was instantly converted into high pressure steam that swept the surface before being forcibly returned to the hydrosphere.

It was a primeval hell that must have prevailed—a spherical hollow cauldron in which the chemicals were stirred and mixed as if by some unseen hand. All the chemicals were there, even sulphur—the brimstone of the Bible—that had found its way from the molten interior of the Earth to the clouds above it.

But that was not all.

This strange, and possibly unstable, soup was then energised by flashes of lightning that razed the sunless earth; was that the hand that mixed the soup?

Within those clouds, under those violent conditions, the amino acids were formed. They are simple organic compounds consisting of two groups of atoms—the carboxyl group, COOH, and the amino group, NH_2. Every one of the constituent elements, that form the amino acids, was already in place, and under the circumstances she has described, the atoms of the two groups came together as a natural way of being!

Is that possible, or is it just speculation? Wishful thinking?

In 1953, S.L. Miller ran an interesting experiment. He put together all of the basic chemicals, together with a few more that were thought to be in the broth at the time, in a flask, and pummeled them with electrical discharges—to simulate the effects of lightning in the upper atmosphere—and synthesised several of the basic amino acids.

But they are not life. We have yet a long way to go.

As we have seen, an amino acid consists of one carboxyl group and one amino group. Under certain conditions, however, the carbon atom of the carboxyl group of one amino acid bonds to the nitrogen atom of the amino group of another amino acid—and we have a 'peptide'.

Two amino acid atoms have bonded to form a molecule. But more of the amino acid atoms can bond in the same way to form a chain. If ten such amino acid atoms bond together, the chain is called an 'oligopeptide'. When fifty such bonds connect fifty amino acid atoms together—we have a 'protein' molecule.

The fundamental, and essential, building blocks of life had appeared on the scene. Not life itself, but the stuff of which life would be made. The polypeptides, as proteins, come in different types depending on the constituent amino acids forming the protein. All contain hydrogen, oxygen, nitrogen, carbon, and nearly all contain some sulphur as well. In addition some protein molecules contain small amounts of phosphorous, iron, zinc, and copper.

Simple proteins contain only amino acids; conjugated proteins, on the other hand, contain other organic and inorganic compounds connected to the amino acids, and the most interesting are the nucleo—proteins. They contain nucleic acids.

The nucleic acids are a group of organic substances found in the chromosomes of living cells and in viruses in combination with the proteins. Put together they become awesome in the storage and replication of hereditary information as in the DNA and the RNA molecule. There are double helix chains of the atoms of these same simple elements connected together, so that the chains may peel off and each can connect with a similar chain from another arrangement—to form a third chain with characteristics from one-half of each of the parent chains.

Matter had found a way to replicate itself!

But how would that hereditary information be carried?

In the genes! And the genes are subunits of the chain called 'nucleotides'. The information carried in the genes is coded in the sequences of the nucleotides—which correspond to the sequences of the amino acids in the polypeptide chain of proteins.

I really don't know what this biochemist is so patiently trying to tell us. Is she trying to convince us that through a simple set of chemical combinations life arose on earth? Or is she trying to tell us that the whole process is so darned complex and involved that the chances of it having actually occurred by itself on Earth, unaided, is well nigh impossible?

That is for us to decide. She is merely placing the evidence before us. But before we can decide, we have to study 'probability'. And for that we need a special type of mathematician. We need a statistician.

Oh, no! Not mathematics! I hated it! It was not my strongest suit, shall we say. You will lose me for sure. Up to now, I have been able to keep up with you, but if you start to delve into mathematics all bets are off !

Relax, good friend. Would I pull that one on you? Make the subject so incomprehensible that the jury is confused? That is for lawyers—not for people of good faith, like us. So, let us bring in the statistician.

Consider the very simple act of tossing a coin. That we both understand, and we'll do it right here on this sidewalk. People may look askance at us—the two of us tossing a penny into the air, but it is for a good cause!

You toss it. Will it come down as 'heads' or will it come down as 'tails' ? The chance of either occurrence is precisely the same—50/50. And every single time you toss the coin, since there are only two alternatives in the toss—heads or tails—the chance that each will occur in that toss is always 50/50. Do you agree?

Yes. I toss it, and it came down 'heads'.

Good! So, now, toss it again. What is the probability that it will come down as 'heads' ? Still 50/50 for the second toss, is it not?

Yes.

But it came down as 'heads' in the first toss. Does it have the same probability of coming down as 'heads' again in the second toss?

Well, I tossed it again—and it did!

True. So toss it one hundred times. If for ninety—nine times it has come down as 'heads', do you still expect that the penny will come down as 'heads' the hundredth time—even though its chance in that hundredth toss is still 50/50?

No. I see what you mean. The chances that 'heads' will be able to repeat the same performance every time becomes slimmer and slimmer with each succeeding toss.

Precisely! So what if I asked you to toss the penny a million times? Would you say there is any possibility, whatsoever, that the penny will still come down as 'heads' the millionth time?

No.

But there is one way in which that could occur.

You're kidding aren't you? After persuading me to admit that there is no possibility, you are now telling me that there is?

Toss the penny again, but before it reaches the ground catch it and then, when no one is looking, make it come 'heads'.

That's cheating!

You could say that you are 'aiding', it? But you see now, don't you, that you could toss it not one million but one billion times and still make it come out 'heads' every single time, could you not?

Yes.

Well there we have it. The choices before us.

Either we have to accept that every one of the events that occurred—the Big Bang, the formation of the atoms, the formation of molecules, the diversification of matter, the formation of the galaxies, the formation of the Milky way and our own Sun, the formation of the Earth, the right conditions on Earth and in the hydrosphere, the first amino acids, the connection of fifty—not one or two but fifty—of the amino acids to form the first protein molecules, the even more complex formulation of the DNA molecule, each event itself comprising of thousands, if not millions, of individual, constituent events—each with their own probability of occurrence, all occurred in the exact and precise sequence in which they occurred, and that led to the origin of life. All by random chance? The probability of that occurring is estimated of the order of one in ten billion!

But it could have.

Or we have to accept that the only possible way in which that sequence of events, that led to the origin of life on Earth, could have occurred, is if it was 'aided'. In which case we have to accept that every one of those events was, in fact, orchestrated with a depth of knowledge that made certain they would occur in the sequence in which they did occur. The origin of life on Earth was a foregone conclusion!

One or the other? There can be no half measures. But wait! Before you decide, let me add one more compelling argument to the total picture.

You sound like that TV commercial urging me to pick up the phone and call a toll—free number. I'm waiting!

We have not considered how life actually began. All we have reached is DNA and RNA. Do you know their definition? DNA is deoxyribonucleic acid. And RNA is ribonucleic acid. They are only acids. DNA is not life! It has the spiral structure that allows it to peel apart and combine with the half that comes from another source—but who does the peeling? That is life! The desire and the will to replicate.

Have you ever sometimes wondered why even the lowest forms of unthinking, unfeeling life—such as the cold virus or bacteria or grass—all have the intense desire and the will to replicate?

What is it that made a straightforward combination of chemical molecules—however complex they might be—to behave differently from other molecules, forcing us to recognise them as the origins of life? Because there is no doubt that life, as we know it, manifests behaviour that is different from that exhibited by inanimate matter—even when the same molecules are synthesised in the laboratory? As we have said, life has reproductive qualities, even if it is merely cell division in the very lowest forms. It has metabolism, growth—and a compelling desire to be alive! That is what defines life in the end—a compelling desire to live and procreate.

How did chemical molecules acquire that compelling desire?

There are two theories that seek to explain the origin of life.

The materialistic theory, held by the mechanistic school of thought, maintains that there is no essential difference between the animate and the inanimate, and that, at the most elementary level of viruses and bacteria, living matter is made up of precisely the same—and only those elements which make up inanimate matter, except that they are differently organised. Organise those very same chemicals, in that very same way, in a laboratory test tube—and the materials will be, automatically, imbibed with that vital spark that causes it to live.

The vitalistic, or animistic, theory holds a view that is a diametrical opposite of the materialistic theory.

It maintains that what distinguishes the living from the non-living is a vital force or spark, without which those same chemicals would be deprived of that compelling desire to be alive.

No matter. Does it really matter whether such a spark exists or does not exist? It has certainly never been proven in a laboratory. It has never been isolated. If it does exist, where does it inhabit the organism? One may cut some worms in two, and have each part walk away from each other! Then were there two sparks? Does it inhabit each and every cell? It must, because even when the organism has died, cells from that organism can be kept alive, and some parts of the organism, such as the kidneys and the eyes of the dead person, can be transplanted into another live person. So the spark must still inhabit those cells. The only chemical molecule, that each and every cell of the organism carries with it, is the genetic code. Is the spark, in some way, intrinsic to the genetic code? Crack the code, synthesise it in a test tube, and if it begins to replicate, the spark has entered it!

But isn't that precisely what the mechanistic school is saying?

The probability of the entire event occurring, without it being conceived, planned and executed as an 'aided' event, is so incredibly small, that whichever theory on the origin of life is correct—is immaterial. Whether the spark spontaneously arose in the DNA or was infused into it does not alter a thing. Would you agree?

Yes.

But there is one massive black hole in the argument. The statement that the probability of this occurrence is infinitely small applies if, and only if, there is just one final event in the origin of life. Here on Earth! If out there in all the galaxies of our universe, with their trillions of stars each with orbiting planets, there is life-based on the protein molecule or on other chemical compounds—the probability argument for an 'aided' event is shattered! The 'probability' no longer applies, because then it has become a 'possibility'.

But there is no other life out there—no nickel men or copper men or women of salt!

Astronomers are quick to dispute this.

Is it not the height of egoism, they say, to suggest that we are the sole inhabitants of this gigantic universe. They point—as I have done—to the millions of galaxies with their trillions of stars. Surely there are other suns with millions of planets like Earth?

Are there others out there? Where is the evidence? We have had television now for about 60 years, and radio for longer than that. The signals from 'The Lucy Show' have been traveling into outer space—at the speed of light—for at least 50 years. Our nearest neighboring star is only three light-years away from us. Any civilisation, at least as advanced as our own, must no doubt have greeted her with great delight. And reciprocated with some show of approval or applause? Perhaps by sending us some programs of their own to delight us in turn?

There have been none.

The entire Milky Way galaxy is 100,000 light-years in diameter, with our sun lying about 30,000 light-years from the center of it. If in all of the galaxy, in those billions of stars, there was even one—just one—civilisation that was 70,000 years ahead of us—and 70,000 years is a miniscule amount in evolutionary time!—we would be hearing not only from our neighboring stars but from the other side of the galaxy.

We have not heard a whisper from anywhere.

We can carry the argument even still further. Consider the Andromeda galaxy. It contains twice as many stars as the Milky Way—200 billion of them. It is barely two million light—years away, with a diameter of about 120,000 light—years. If in all of the Andromeda galaxy there was even one civilisation—just one—that was two million years more advanced than we are—and even two million years is no more than one brief minute in evolutionary time—we would have heard from them. For sure!

And we have not.

But what if, the astronomers say, those civilisations are not more advanced than we are?

Is it not the height of egoism to suggest that we are the most advanced civilisation in the billions of planets circling the billions of stars that form all the galaxies in this universe?

light years from the center of it. If in all of the galaxy, in those billions of stars, there was even one spot, one civilization that was 50,000 years ahead of us—and 50,000 years is a mere flick, a moment, in astronomy time!—we would be hearing not only from our neighboring stars but from the other side of the galaxy.

We have not heard a whisper from anywhere.

We can carry the argument even still further. Consider the Andromeda galaxy. It contains twice as many stars as the Milky Way—200 billion of them. It is barely two million light years away with a diameter of about 120,000 light years. If in all of the Andromeda galaxy there was even one civilization—just one—that was two million years more advanced than we are—and even two million years is no more than one brief minute in astronomical time—we would have heard from them for sure.

And we have not.

But what if, the astronomers say, these civilizations are not more advanced than we are?

Is it not the height of conceit to suggest that we are the most advanced civilization in the billions of planets circling the billions of stars that form the galaxies in the universe?

7

Evolutionary Biology

May I suggest that we not break for lunch today?

Oh! Why? I have no problems having lunch with you, but why, on this fourth day, did you think of it?

We are starting a little later than usual. It is almost eleven o'clock. We are going to hear, today, evidence from the evolutionary biologist. She is also a microbiologist. It is a very painful story that she will tell us, but to understand it with compassion, I would like us to have the complete picture in one sitting. Besides, the Indian restaurant, next door to this café, has been wafting its titillating, spicy aromas onto the sidewalk, and driving me to distraction! Let me treat you today; perhaps, you can treat me tomorrow?

Done!

Lamb biryani for me. It will come with a yoghurt raitha. What would you like?

They make a great tandoori chicken. I've eaten here before.

Some type of vegetable? Spinach?

No!

Cauliflower with potatoes?

Great!

Ah! There she is. Why, she is in a sari! Well, let us find out what the dear girl wants, and we can talk as we eat.

The first life on Earth are the viruses. Tough little pests! The virus is an entity that hovers in between life and death. It is neither dead nor alive. It does not respire, will not grow, needs no food, cannot think or feel, and whose sole fun in life, so it seems, is to infect its host! But when it does, it performs its sole function in life—which is to reproduce. That it does by injecting its nucleic acid into the cell of the host; then uses the chemical energy of the host cell and its protein synthesising capabilities to replicate itself.

So the world's first living organism is a parasite!

I think you judge it too harshly. It does not see itself as a parasite. It has not the means to reproduce itself; must it then be denied the fundamental, biological urge of reproduction?

Which poses the first question in biology.

Why do living organisms possess the urge to reproduce—even down to the simplest viruses? The microbiologist in her will tell us that the urge to reproduce is the first primeval urge—more fundamental and basic than even the instinct for individual survival. And, as any twelve-year-old will be pleased to tell us, the will to be can only be fulfilled if it is accompanied by the will to continue to be!

Tough, little things—the viruses. And yet, perhaps, they demonstrate more than any other living organism the fundamental nature of life itself. They can stand boiling temperatures and freezing ones. Some can withstand radiation; some can survive for thousands of years without ill-effects, only to come to life again and replicate themselves when a suitable host becomes available. They have the will to multiply! Because they have no life—sustaining mechanisms, they quite simply become non-life when it suits them.

A virus balances on the edge between chemistry and biology as a protein molecule with a genetic strand running through it. So the next time you have a cold, do by all means cover yourself warmly, drink warm soup, and cuddle up into a warm bed. But give yourself some satisfaction by reflecting that the tiny organism that is making your life so miserable came into being in the hydrosphere above Earth, when the barbaric conditions on the surface of it made Earth an inferno.

And there it hung for the billion or so years that were yet to pass, unwilling to die, cheating death by the simple expedient of playing a chemical molecule within the clouds. Waiting for the right time when the conditions would be favourable for it to descend to the surface of Earth.

This is where her story as an evolutionary biologist begins. There was no free oxygen in the clouds. It had all been used up to form the water vapor. So the first organisms on Earth were anaerobic—did not need oxygen for survival. Another billion years were to pass before the appearance of green algal stromatolites that, lying in the oceans, produced abundant oxygen by the process of photosynthesis.

The process is really quite simple. Algae is green; it contains a chemical called chlorophyll that it exposes to the sunlight. Moisture is drawn up from the roots and transported as sap to the chlorophyll. The carbon dioxide in the atmosphere is absorbed by the plant, and the chlorophyll, in the presence of sunlight, breaks up the water into hydrogen and oxygen. Carbon combines with the hydrogen, together with some of the oxygen, to form a carbohydrate—so essential for the survival of the plant. That is 'food' for the plant. It manufactures its own food from water, the atmosphere and sunlight! But what is more important from our point of view is that the remaining oxygen is released into the atmosphere—for all of us!

It was the availability of that free oxygen released into the atmosphere that led to the evolution of higher organisms—as in the Animal Kingdom.

As yet, we have no quarrel with evolution. A tree merely stands in one place and breathes. It turns its thousands of solar collectors to the sunlight and manufactures carbohydrates. That is all the food the tree needs to live. Because it then modifies the carbohydrates into glucose, fats, proteins, starches, cellulose and anything else it needs for growth, survival or repair. Brilliant wouldn't you say?

I would.

And it does not even have to be a tree. Everything 'green' performs just as well! Moss, lichen, grass and weeds—the ones you put pesticide on—all of them help to put oxygen into the atmosphere for our survival.

Were it not for the botanical structures in the Plant Kingdom none of us three would be here today.

Then why is she so depressed? She has given us uplifting evidence.

True. As yet. It is what comes after that makes her weep.

We cannot go into all of evolutionary history—however charming our guest may be—because it is the fundamental questions that need answering, and that trouble us so, that we need to ask. The answers we receive will guide our thinking on the true nature of God.

What are the arguments for evolution being part of his scheme and purpose, and so of his doing?

What are the arguments that the results of evolution, as we see them around us, can only lead us to the conclusion that he withdrew from it? Or at the very least that he failed in it!

Strong words! This is blasphemy, unless you can produce the evidence to substantiate that conclusion.

Evolution is a sad story. It could have been so different, and it is not. The evolution of botanical organisms—with a few exceptions such as parasitic plants or the Venus fly-trap-leaves us with no reason to criticise. But a line of differentiation had already occurred early in evolutionary history. One such line led to the Plant Kingdom; the other led to the Animal Kingdom. Both were in the sea.

It is with the Animal Kingdom that our unhappiness lies.

Whereas the Plant Kingdom would, for the most part, be able to manufacture its own food for growth and survival—with which we have no quarrel—from non-living matter, the Animal Kingdom came to the devastating realisation that, for growth and survival, some members of the Animal Kingdom would need to eat other weaker members of that same kingdom—sometimes even weaker members of their own species!

Only one law would determine evolutionary history.

Survival of the fittest!

To survive and grow, every individual organism in the Animal Kingdom has to eat. Life has to eat life.

Predator and prey!

Whether you are a non-vegetarian predator—as we are; you are eating chicken and I am eating lamb—or a vegetarian as she is, eating cauliflower and potatoes, we are all eating some form of a living organism. The ones we—you and I—are eating had a nervous system and so we caused pain to the poor creatures when they were slaughtered. The vegetables she is eating did not have a nervous system, and so were not caused pain when they were harvested. But the principle is still the same. Life is eating life for survival and growth.

Was that really necessary? Survival of the fittest!

If you are fit, you will survive. If you survive, you were fit. If you are not fit, you will not survive. If you did not survive, sorry, but you were unfit!

Is that a moral law? To determine who shall live and who shall die?

No other law would dominate the growth, survival and evolution of species that led, by genetic mutation, from jawless fish in the sea, to fish with jaws and lobes, to amphibians, and then to reptiles. The line then bifurcates, one branch leading to the birds and the other to mammals and us.

The branch that leads to the birds is fairly straight; the branch that leads to us is not.

For us, evolutionary history is complex with many dead ends. So many thousands of species had to suffer for us to survive.

Surely you are being too harsh, aren't you? I understand that some became extinct, but it was not for our survival?

Then let the entomologist tell us his story. About the insects. Next to us and the primates, they are quite simply the most intelligent creatures alive. The social insects, like the termites, have superb organisational skills that have allowed them to practice farming, agriculture, build termitaries with fungus gardens, well-ventilated—in some cases with actual chimneys to exhaust the hot air—and some of them over 10 feet tall. Body size to body size, we would have to build a skyscraper a mile high to equal the achievements of the termites!

A queen termite lays about 30,000 eggs in a single day. Most insects have a fantastic rate of reproduction which makes them, quite simply, the most successful breeding machines ever made!

So? I don't see cause for complaint.

Have you ever wondered why they are so abundant, and yet so low down on the ecological pyramid? There are more than 700,000+ species of insects—some new ones are being discovered every year!—yet they lie just one level above the grasses that provide food to the herbivores. Have you ever wondered why?

He is going to tell us anyway.

Yes. Because insects did not develop lungs! Their oxygen intake is so small—some primitive insects breathe directly through the body wall—that it ruled out the development of insects of large size. If insects had developed lungs, a beetle would have been the size of a Volkswagen motor car! With a large size, fantastic breeding rates, and their superb social skills, there is no doubt they would have decimated their enemies and very easily established themselves at the top of the ecological pyramid. As it was, all they could accomplish in the complex scheme of evolution was to be food for the insectivores! At about the time that they became abundant food supply, there also evolved an insectivorous rodent—nothing but a common rat—that, finding such ample food supply, was able to strengthen its chances for survival in a hostile environment.

This primitive insectivorous rodent was a mammal.

This insectivorous mammal evolved into a multitude of species that include, among others, the mammoths, rabbits, carnivores and the primates.

The primates lead to us. There are so very many questions we have to ask and answer; where shall we start?

Is 'man' at the top of the evolutionary pyramid?

I think we can hardly dispute that. We are in the driver's seat. We may not be very good drivers and we have been responsible for great harm to other species, but the fact that we can control them, harm them, eat them—this lamb is truly succulent meat; how's your chicken?—kill them for sport too, must surely be unequivocal proof that we are in the driver's seat. If you need statistical proof, that too is available.

In the Animal Kingdom, we have identified 700,000+ species of insects, 55,000+ species of spiders and scorpions, 30,000+ species of fish, 8600+ species of birds, 6500+ species of reptiles, 4100+ species of mammals, one species of man. Three races, but, mercifully, only one species, so that all the three races can breed, freely, each with the other.

Yes, we are undoubtedly at the top of the ecological and evolutionary pyramid.

But was that the intent of evolution?

Ah! There we do have a problem. Because the evolutionary biologists don't agree with each other. One theory states quite categorically that this was a random occurrence! There is no evidence, they say, that evolution was designed to place 'man' at the very top of the ecological pyramid—and yet, that is where we are.

But was it God's intent to place us there? How could he possibly have accomplished that if, as we have agreed, he used his own existing energy to form the universe and is now immersed in it? He was not there to 'aid' the course of evolutionary history over the many billion years that were to pass; he was right here!

May I run a scenario past you?

I'm beginning to be extremely distrustful of your scenarios!

Oh, come now! Have I ever swung anything past you, or over you? All I do is to provide the scenario and let you be the judge of whether it was possible or not.

Very well.

Imagine that you are standing at the top of a staircase and at the very bottom of the stairs is a small bucket. In your hand is a small green ball. The object of the exercise is to get the green ball into the bucket. Do you get the picture?

Yes.

Let us also say that you know all of physics—you made the laws; so that could hardly be a problem! So it would be easy for you to determine the exact speed and force with which you would drop the green ball so that, knowing the resilience of the green ball and the hardness of the stairs, the green ball bounces on the first step, then on the fourth, then again on the thirtieth step—and lands in the bucket. Would it not?

Yes.

Well now, let us make the problem a little bit more difficult. Assume that the staircase is not a straight one but partly spiral, partly curved, even—like a roller coaster—going sometimes down and sometimes up, with the small bucket at the very last step!

Impossible! No law of physics could achieve that!

Not true. Suppose you then decide to start of with many more balls than just the green ball. You have a hundred, if necessary a thousand or a million balls to bounce off the first step. The objective is still the same; put the green ball into the bucket, but it will need help at many crucial points in its path. That is obvious even to the both of us. So you can work out, how many other criss—crossing, secondary staircases you will need, and with what force to drop each of the thousand other balls, with differing resilience—but all at the exact same time that you drop the green ball!

As your primary staircase starts to spiral away, the green ball would—on its own have been unable to go with it. Unless at that precise instant of time, a brown ball arrives to nudge the green ball, thereby applying the course correction to 'aid' the green ball on its way to the bucket. Every single time, when it seems as if the green ball will lose its way, a red ball, or a white ball, or a yellow ball, or a hundred other such balls are there at just the right time and at just the right spot to aid your green ball into the bucket. You could even toss a blue ball into the air so that it comes down a million years later at the right time and at the right spot to nudge the green ball toward the bucket. Yet, once you released all the balls you were not there to oversee how they behaved, were you? They behaved according to the laws of physics and chemistry and biology—including insects not developing lungs but providing an abundant food supply to our mammal rodent, or a meteor impact wiping out the dinosaurs, or any other of the thousand other events that have shaped evolutionary history—to put 'man' in the driver's seat.

At the very least it is more credible a scenario than suggesting that it was all 'random', is it not?

Yes.

He does not have to be 'there' for it to be still according to his will?

But then you have arrived at 'determinism', have you not? Everything is pre-ordained; we have no free will! Do we even know who we are? What exactly is the relationship between this animal body of mine and me? You are shifting the responsibility for all the miserable state of affairs we have on this planet onto his shoulders, are you not? Is that fair? Is that not blasphemy?

Not, if there is purpose and meaning... .

Is there purpose and meaning?

Why don't we wait until all the evidence is in before we answer that question? But it is an appropriate time, now, for us to consider all the other questions you have hurled at me. We will bring in the neurologist.

8

Me and My Body: The 'Knower' and 'Free Will'

I notice you said 'this animal body of mine and me'. Was that deliberate? Because you are so right! When I say 'my body' it is as if I am not speaking of myself but of some alien creature quite distinct from me that I inhabit. Let me set the record straight. I have a body that biological evolution has placed me in. I can't say I'm always compatible with it or it with me. We have our disagreements, but I'd say that on the whole we get on very well. It isn't a grotesque body; neither is it stunning. Just average; the sort I don't parade, but of which I am not ashamed either.

How did I arrive at this body?

In early evolution, every cell was an independent entity—as in single-celled organisms. The cell's only goal was survival. It is fairly well documented that single cells, intent only on survival, will take nutrition away from other cells if they have to. They are not noble or self-sacrificing or even ethical about it! There is no moral law governing their behaviour.

When they evolved into more complex organisms—for their own survival—there had to be some 'order' rather than a 'free-for-all'. In other words, those organisms that developed 'order' were more likely to work toward the common good of the organism, and hence their own survival in a hostile environment.

Darwin's theory of natural selection.

When such organisms became even more complex, it became clear that they needed more than just 'order'; they needed a 'controller'. At first, this controller was merely a relay station. Consider four cells, A, B, C, and D that have to feedback messages to each other for their common good. The messages had to be collected, organised, redistributed through the relay. But what if the feedback demand from A to D was detrimental to the health of B ? The controller had to exercise control to ensure that all such individual demands being made were not harmful to the organism as a whole.

So, perhaps much against their will, the controller was given some powers other than merely the relaying of feedback messages—and that is me! It was the power to make decisions based on the information presented to it that gave rise to an 'I'. Notice, I said 'an' I and not 'the' I. Because the cells forming the organism did not yield unconditional control. They realised that certain basic processes, needed to keep them alive, should be kept out of the control of the controller!

Such as?

Such as the beating of the heart, or the functioning of vital organs such as the lungs or the liver. These functions were still retained under the control of a separate controller, with no powers other than to respond to feedback mechanisms, in set responses that were not subject to a capricious rearrangement. This is the 'involuntary' controller, or the animal brain. The 'voluntary' controller is me.

However, organisms that did have some sort of 'voluntary' controller, capable of making independent decisions, were more successful to adapting to changes in the environment, or unusual circumstances—and so were better able to survive, and pass on their genes to their offspring. It gave the organism flexibility to respond to emergency situations.

Let us say I have torn a muscle in my left leg while being chased by a tiger! The feedback mechanisms from my left leg will categorically demand that the body cease to put any more stress on it, and relays this information in no uncertain terms, by signals of severe pain, to the 'involuntary' controller, who passes it on to me. But with the tiger breathing down my neck, I am hardly likely to respond to such feedback signals—even at the risk of losing the entire left leg to eventual amputation! The 'voluntary' controller (I) decided that the loss of the left leg was preferable to becoming meal for the tiger!

In evolution, as of now, that is the status quo that has been reached. Part of my body responds to involuntary control from the animal brain. I really have no idea of how my liver functions or what my gall bladder is doing at this moment—and quite frankly, my dear, I don't give a damn!—but they had better be doing what they are supposed to be doing, for otherwise I won't feel well. I will then give it some foul tasting medicine or have it surgically removed or whatever. But I have been given control of some functions, such as where I shall move, and when I do move shall I run or shall I walk, shall I feed this body in response to its hunger signals, and with what? Lamb or tandoori chicken or a cauliflower and potato vegetable?

It is this voluntary control and the exercise of it that constitutes the 'I'. It cannot be a feedback mechanism, because feedback mechanisms, and actions based on them, are for the good of the organism. Yet I can take actions that violate every feedback signal being input to me and are, quite distinctly, not for the good of the body! An example is suicide. Since every cell will fight for survival, as a natural instinct, regardless of the circumstances; there is no situation in which the biological organism can possibly decide, on its own, that death is the preferred alternative—had it been merely responding to feedback mechanisms. In that case, even slow and lingering death, with part or parts of the organism dying, would still have feedback from other parts demanding that the organism continue to survive—regardless of the consequences!

Yet, voluntarily, and in good health, rational people have chosen to ignore the good of the entire biological organism—and commit suicide.

This suggests that in the evolutionary process, the controller has gone from relay station, to a controller with limited interpretive powers, to the animal controller with full control over the involuntary functions so necessary for the day-to-day survival of the body—and me! I have no control over the animal functions so necessary for my day-to-day survival—such as the beating of my heart or the flow of blood through my veins—even if I knew how, which I don't. What I can do, however, is to interfere with those functions by external action—such as by cutting the vein in my left leg, much to the detriment of my body.

It is a very fragile relationship that I have established with my body. It can make me feel very sick and give me considerable pain, if I abuse my power. It can even die on me!

On the other hand, it is not me! It gave rise to me—and I could not possibly exist without it.

So who, and what, exactly is me?

The 'I' of me?

To understand that better, we have to discuss the 'knower' and 'identity'. It is quite obvious that a person 'knows'. So he is capable of 'knowing'. But the actual act of 'knowing', and the 'knower', has never been fully understood. Some neurologists have stated, categorically, that the 'knower' may never be known. Yet, it is there in each and every single one of us! Not outside us; but right there within us. So why should the 'knower' never be capable of being 'known'? Because it then becomes a matter of 'identity'.

There are two possibilities regarding the 'knower'.

It is possible that the 'knower' or the mechanism that knows, is merely a group of cells, or parts of the brain, that contain the DNA—like every other cell—but whose sole function is to 'know'. It is also the seat of identity, so that the 'knower' is 'Dandekar'. Now let me run a scary scenario past you.

Oh, no!

Let us say that two men die in an accident at the precise same time and in close proximity to one another—and I am one of them. The other is X.

Oh, please! Must we have such gruesome scenarios?

Bear with me. The end may not be so tragic after all. My entire body and all of my organs are destroyed, but only those brain cells that constitute the 'knower', and hence my identity, survive intact. In X only those very same brain cells destroyed, but his body and all his organs survive intact. The surgeons, swiftly before death occurs to all of the organs or brain cells, surgically are able to implant my brain cells into X's brain. Do you get the picture?

Perfectly!

The possibility we have considered that the 'knower' and identity are one and the same would imply that my identity would be transferred to X, so that I wake up from the surgery with my own identity intact. I will awaken in X, but as me! However, will I awaken with my memory banks intact? So that I remember that I had lamb for lunch—and carry on this conversation with you tomorrow as if nothing had changed. You would see a different body—but it would still be me!

Or will I awaken with my identity connected to X's memory banks, thereby remembering what X had for lunch, but totally ignorant of what I had for lunch. I would not turn up for our meeting tomorrow, because, quite simply I don't know who you are, or that we had this conversation here at all!

The second possibility is more intriguing and, in my opinion, far more realistic.

Let us say that the 'knower' is independent of the identity of the person—and identical in every single individual. A sort of generic 'record player', so that if you connect the 'knower' to my memory banks—it is me! Connect that same 'knower' to X's memory banks and it is X!

What is so very interesting—and I would not hesitate to add a few more 'very's' to the sentence above—is that resurrection becomes a scientific reality! Record and store my memory banks in some biological, or electronic or 'other' format—and, it is possible that, at this very moment, this very conversation is being recorded and stored somewhere, either within me or outside me—and my identity is preserved for ever. Because I am my memory banks. After I am dead; what else am I? No further experiences are possible. All that is necessary then is for a universal 'knower' to 'play' me, and my identity will come to life again.

May I say something?

Please do.

You are mad! Quite simply a lunatic—if there ever was one! How I could have agreed to spending time—wasting it—with you, is beyond my comprehension! I must be a lunatic too. But, please, please, would you continue?

Thanks. I will. Call me what you will, but I am only setting forth the scientific evidence—and it will take us where it will. We will not flinch from the truth. That was our agreement—and I will hold you to it!

Pray, proceed. Though you may notice that our neurologist has departed in a huff! I don't blame him; I very nearly did so myself.

Well, since you are in such a receptive mood, and since you did ask, a while ago, about 'free will', this is the appropriate time for us to discuss it.

Do we have a free will?

It depends on what you mean by the word 'free'.

That sort of ambiguity is not permitted. Do we have free will or not?

First, before we consider free will, let us consider 'decision-making' capability. We are capable of making decisions—but then so are lower forms of life, including trees.

You're joking, of course!

I'm deadly serious. The true example I can give is of a silver maple that grows in my backyard; I planted it myself as a sapling. It did well and grew taller. Then, one day, the single trunk of the tree suffered some sort of damage—it could be frost damage or wind damage or animal damage, I'm not sure. But that it was damaged, a foot or so above the ground was very clear. A few days later, the tree produced a small branch from below the damaged section. The branch from below the damaged section continued to prosper very rapidly, and soon became the main trunk of the silver maple. In time, the original diseased trunk fell off, but the damage at the junction is still visible to the naked eye.

Since the sapling could not have known—when planted—that it was going to suffer damage, it had to make the decision to start another branch below the damaged section, when it realised that the damage it had suffered would not permit the original trunk of the tree to grow and prosper. Wouldn't you agree?

Yes.

Well, does that not demonstrate decision-making ability? I would say it does. Does that mean the tree has free will? No, of course not! We should not confuse a decision-making capability with free will.

Now let me run a scenario past you—one of my simpler ones!

Let us say that you have a dog chained at the collar, with a ten foot leash having a steel ring at the other end that is slipped over a steel post embedded into the ground. Get the picture?

Yes.

Within a radius of ten feet, the dog is perfectly free to do whatever he wishes. He can sit, stand, bark, walk, run in circles, even fraternise with other dogs if they come within his circle of influence.

But would you say that the dog is free? I think not.

In just the same way, each one of us is born with our own genetic, hereditary characteristics, and live under differing environmental conditions and circumstances. The genetic characteristics, for example, may dictate that you have a very placid personality; I may have a very temperamental one! You were born into a very wealthy family, perhaps? I come from an upper middle-class one. Within the restraints laid down for us, we do have the 'free will' to make decisions, but our decisions will be different because we are also prisoners to our own 'leash'. Every living organism is on a 'leash'! Then, do we have free will? By its definition, the word 'free' does not permit of even one single constraint placed on it. The true test of free will is this: given the same information, you and I would reach precisely the same decision—if we were both independent of the hereditary and other restraints imposed on us. That we reach different decisions must imply that neither one of us is truly free.

I wish I had run away from you when I had the chance to do so. Now, I am desolate. And lost! Why do you do this to me?

Well, then, to increase your misery, let me put before you one last scenario on this subject, and then you can tell me whether you agree with me or not.

I hear you groan in agony, but I will continue nevertheless.

A baker in India has put his wares—all of them about to expire for legal sale so that he would be forced to throw them away—on a table outside his bakery. All the 'goodies'—the cakes, pies, muffins—have been sold. There remains one last loaf of stale bread, priced at one rupee; so he leaves the table unattended to attend to more important business in the bakery.

Two children—same race, same age—stand in front of the table and eye the loaf of bread.

The child on the left—who was looking for any remaining muffins-sniffs his nose and walks away. He will go home to a dinner of chicken curry with rice and potatoes, with a glass of warm milk, topped by a dessert of mango ice cream.

The child on the right eyes the loaf with intense longing. He will go home to three hungry siblings, and, if their mother—who is out on the streets begging—does manage to get in a few rupees, they will eat; otherwise they go hungry for the night. He grabs the loaf of stale bread and runs for it.

Tell me, my friend, did either child have free will?

Does any of us have 'free' will?

Only God has free will.

9

Predator and Prey: The First Emotion of Fear

I do not know whether you will come today. After that stormy session we had yesterday evening, I cannot be sure. Of anything.

You called me mad! Perhaps, I am. It has not been easy for me either. I have struggled with this train of thought for the past twenty years. Yes, twenty years! Fighting myself, at every step along the way, to accept the series of logical conclusions, each dictating the next; all dictated by the very first.

The origin—not of the species—but of the Laws of Physics! The ability of simple elementary particles, all forms of energy, to diversify into matter in such a simple way. The ability of life, by genetic mutation, to diversify, over time, into the rich variety of life forms that we have today.

I feel your hand on my shoulder as you slip into the seat beside me.

I'm sorry.

No problem.

So who do you have for me today?

The psychologist.

Ah! So you do think we are both mad, don't you?

On the contrary; he—more than anyone else—will help us out of this quagmire of doubt in which we find ourselves. We reach conclusions dictated by logic, but which we then cannot accept—neither intellectually nor emotionally—as the truth.

Emotion!

That is what it is all about. That is what he is going to talk to us about today. What is emotion?

Loosely defined it means feeling. In psychology, however, emotion is defined as a response to a specific stimulus. Fear, for instance, is a response to danger. The stimulus initiates characteristic changes in the physiology of the body, including change in the pulse rate, rise in body temperature, change in the breathing rate, greater or lesser secretions from certain glands, and, perhaps, as a result of all this, the release of specific chemicals, which, as they reach the cognitive part of the brain, induce the emotion of fear. The organism then takes appropriate action to relieve itself of it. This action could involve fleeing from the predator—or fighting it!

Fear is the first emotion. It was nature's way of warning the creature that it was being threatened and to take evasive action—for survival. Even the lowest of biological organisms in the Animal Kingdom show some rudimentary form of fear. Yet, viruses and bacteria show no fear; neither do algae or plants in the Plant Kingdom. So it is only in the Animal Kingdom that organisms exhibit the emotion of fear to the stimulus of danger.

For survival, fear had to become instinctive. It had to be genetically ingrained in the organism; it was not a learned response. The development of fear, as an instinct, was the blue ball that would give the green ball a nudge, for the survival of biological organisms in the Animal Kingdom, both as individuals and as species, for the evolutionary process to continue—that would, in the end, put the green ball in the bucket—and us on Earth.

Putting emotion into stone could not have been easy. Had there been any other way to do it, I am certain that an entity that had all knowledge would have chosen paths other than the agony—filled principle—that required animals to eat each other! Insectivores, carnivores, cannibals, in the lower organisms of the evolutionary tree, were all necessary to make fear into an instinctive emotion for their survival. It was that requirement for biological food, and only that one requirement, that led to the development of fear as the very first instinctive emotion. If you do not agree, look around you. Energy cannot feel, inanimate matter cannot feel, the Protista Kingdom cannot feel, the Plant Kingdom cannot feel; only the Animal Kingdom has developed the ability to feel.

There are three primary emotions. Fear, love, and anger. All three are now instinctive, in varying degree, in the Animal Kingdom. The billing and cooing of two doves is a rudimentary form of love. The roar of a lion can arise out of the anger it feels at losing its mate. But in the instinctive stage, these are gross emotions, though so very essential—I would say imperative—in the early stages for the survival of the species.

Were it not for the instinctive maternal love that arises in a female bird to feed and care for her little ones—she will fight to the death to protect them—the species could never propagate and survive.

Each emotion, now, has a range of feeling and expression. Love, for instance, can range from ecstatic joy arising out of unbridled affection, to the other extreme of an all-consuming hate. There are subtle shades in between these two extremes; the mid-point could be rated as 'indifference'. Human emotion is both instinctive and 'learned'. Maternal love for the baby is instinctive; the emotion of joy that arises when holding the baby for the first time is a learned emotion. In learned emotions, the same stimulus can cause differing expressions of the same emotion at different stages in the life of the individual. In learned emotions, two individuals from differing cultures, presented with the same stimulus, display different ranges of the same emotion—and in some cases even different emotions!

For example, in our species more than in any other species in the Animal Kingdom, we have the ability to create a work of art that gives the artist joy and fulfillment. What is even more important is that the work of art is capable of communicating that joy to other members of the same species—in her lifetime and beyond it.

The emotion that she has created—and continues to create long after she is dead—does not fall within the purview of fear, love or anger.

In other words, we are capable of creating new emotions, all rooted in joy, that are neither instinctive nor genetic, which are culture oriented, and which represent a quantum leap in biological evolution.

Are there other emotions that are 'learned' emotions that we would do well to cultivate, and pray that such emotions will, one day, be instinctive?

Let me run the final scenario past you.

I'm beginning to welcome your scenarios.

Not this one, you won't!

Have you ever seen an insectivorous bird eat a grasshopper? I have—on the patio in my backyard. The bird hovers around the grasshopper which is permitted only short hops in its desperate attempt to flee. The bird pecks at the grasshopper, misses it twice, but on the third attempt, succeeds in dislodging a leg. The grasshopper, now, cannot even hop! The bird then pecks off a little morsel of the grasshopper's juicy body and, sitting on my patio, proceeds to enjoy his delicacy—quite oblivious to the writhing grasshopper. It then returns to the grasshopper for another morsel. There is no need for the bird to finish off the insect and put it out of its misery—death is a welcome end to the suffering insect—simply because it knows that the grasshopper cannot flee. I have to tell you that I went out on to the patio, shooed the bird away, and squashed the grasshopper under my shoe. When I had moved away, the bird did return for the now dead insect—so it was not deprived of its kill.

What the bird did not have is 'compassion'.

Compassion is a learned emotion. In my humble opinion, compassion is the highest morality! We would be incapable of wrongdoing if compassion were to become an instinctive emotion. We would be quite incapable of killing someone, or committing adultery, or stealing, or giving false testimony against a neighbor, or coveting his wife and his property, or dishonoring our parents, would we not?

But then, I did say, did I not, that we are a work in progress?

10

A Meaning and Purpose to this Universe

You have gone on an on these past five days. Today is the sixth day, and every time that I ask the question, you prevaricate, postpone, plead to be allowed to present new evidence. But you don't give me an answer!

Answer me—why?

Please, give me one more day—just one more day, today—to present the final piece of evidence, and I give you my word that at the end of the day, I will try to answer your question—based on the evidence. You may not agree, but that is for you to decide. Please?

There are six people on the sidewalk; three men and three women. Scruffy! Dirty clothes! Unwashed and unfed! Are they going to be your evidence?

Yes. The two men are musicians—the sort you see at any street corner. One plays a fiddle; the other a flute. One woman is a street dancer, who dances to their music. The other is a singer; she has a very sweet voice! When they need rest, the third woman will read to us from her poetry.

And who is that man on the sidewalk who seems to be measuring us with his charcoal pencil?

He is an artist who is painting the both of us. So look your best! They will be passing the hat around when they are through, so be compassionate, and dig as deep into your wallet as you can—and I will too.

It has been a very memorable performance, wouldn't you say? For three hours now, this group of artists has enthralled us with song and music, dance, poetry, and presented us with our portraits as well. A small crowd has collected to be with us. The café owner saw a rise in his business on the sidewalk café. He has taken all the artists in to feed them—for free! The hat was passed around; both you and I were generous—as were others in the audience—and the morning has ended to our utmost satisfaction. Wouldn't you agree?

Yes. But you still haven't answered my question.

I thought that was pretty obvious.

Not to me! We answered the how, the who, the what with, the when! We did not answer why it was necessary for God to have done what he did—inflicting so much cruelty on us all. The meaning! The purpose! You said there was one—and I believed you.

Let us go back to God before he set the universe in motion—raised the temperature of all that energy that was him, by fractions of a degree that resulted in the Big Bang. There was nothing else but him. Yet the psychologist was specific about emotion. It can arise only if there is a stimulus. That stimulus arises out of the interaction we have with each other, with objects in space, with memories in time—there has to be something for emotion to be created. And he had none. Because there was nothing else—no space, no time, no universe!

But if had all knowledge—the laws of Physics tell us that he did, and we have already conceded that he had—then he must have known about emotion. The joy that can arise out of it! Can you imagine, even for one moment, how barren an existence we would suffer if we were incapable of feeling? Say it was taken away from us right now—the capacity to feel—even then with the memory of past emotions, of loved ones, of plays we saw or operas we heard, of the aroma of roses, we could still survive. But what if we had no such memories of past emotions and no capacity to feel; only the knowledge that such joy could exist? Would we then not consider it worthwhile to subject ourselves to limitless pain to realise that dream?

The way was clear. Simple too. Create a universe, making sure that matter could diversify, because only diversification would permit the interaction that is so necessary to the creation of emotion. He had to find a way to create diversification, not only in inanimate matter, but in life as well—after he had 'aided' it into being—by genetic mutation, so that the multitude of life forms would give the little nudges necessary to put the green ball into the bucket—and us on Earth.

How do you ensure that species will survive, and in their race to survive generate the first emotion as well. The first emotion—raw fear! Ensure that dog eats dog! Cruel as it may seem—and it is—I submit to you that there could have been no other way—or he would have taken it. Could there have been some other way? If you discount the supposition that he could have waved a wand and made it happen, there is no other way. To put emotion into inanimate elementary particles is no mean feat—even if the process was very cruel. But with it came other emotions too. Wonderful emotions such as a mother's love for her infant—also arising out of the same principle that survival of the species required propagation of the species.

You have the right to ask the question as to whether in his effort to acquire the ability to feel, God was justified in subjecting all of us to the cruelty that would result. With all the knowledge he had—and remember he had all knowledge—it is not possible that he was unaware of the suffering he would put live organisms—us included—through, in his momentous journey to acquire feeling.

Until you rephrase the question. Did he have the right to subject himself to all that cruelty, pain and suffering, in his effort to acquire the ability to feel.

He did have that right.

So you are saying that I am God?

The knower in you—the one that feels the pain and suffering, and is independent of your identity—is him. In all of us! We said, did we not, that there was nothing but him before the universe came into being? So why should we be excluded from being a part of him?

You are a lunatic! Insane, past the point of no return! I refuse to listen to you any longer; the conclusions you have reached make a mockery of our society, of our laws, even of our morality!

Compassion is the highest morality. Do you have a problem with that?

No! But to equate the actions of the two children—the one that walked away from the loaf of bread and the other that stole it—as both being acts of a benign God, is to sanction all the evil in this world as being of his design! That he knew about evil, and did nothing to stop it. That he was aware of the pain and massive suffering that he would inflict on each of us—on every organism ever born—because he ordained that life would eat life in order to survive. Did he create death too for just that same purpose? Far better that he be never able to feel, never have any of the memories that we hold so dear, because he has created us to enjoy such memories—and then just lets us die, some under the most gruesome conditions! Does he need all organisms to be born and to die for that same purpose too? So that he could feel the sadness of it? Of loved ones no more, because he could not feel the sadness of it? That is blasphemy! You should be ashamed of yourself!

I hang my head in shame and despair—because you are so right.

I can only beg his forgiveness.

Epilogue: How Will It All End?

The 'courtroom' is empty. The sidewalk on which we heard the evidence from knowledgeable experts in their own fields is now deserted. They were so eager to teach us all they knew, we had to cut many of them short. I hope we did not offend them. Physicist and astronomer, chemist, biochemist and microbiologist, evolutionary biologist and entomologist, neurologist, psychologist, and finally our set of street musicians with singer and dancer, poet and painter—all men and women of goodwill—told us their enthralling stories.

We listened to them all; then we parted. You did not even shake my hand. You grabbed the book off the table as you left. I don't know what you will do with it.

If you bought it from a bookstore, you could return it and get your money back. If it came from a library shelf, you will return it, with some caustic comments to the librarian, no doubt, on the quality of the books that she provides to the reading public! If it was bought at an annual library garage sale for ten cents—remember all the books you could fit into a grocery bag cost one dollar—you could place it in the trash can on your way home, with no great loss.

The owner of the café is standing beside me with a tray in his hand. On the tray are three steaming cups of tea—with a little milk and sugar—three chicken sandwiches and three glasses of orange juice. He places the tray on the table and sits down.

I don't understand.

First, let me apologise to you and your friend for eavesdropping! My counter is just on the other side of that window behind you. As you raised your voices in heated debate, it was impossible not to hear all that transpired. I'm sorry! I've been sitting at my register, glued to it for the past six days, entranced by all the evidence that I have heard. So compelling were the stories, I upset both my wife and daughter by ignoring my duties in my café! As a peace offering may I offer you a light supper of a chicken sandwich with a glass of orange juice and a cup of tea—the way you've been ordering it these past six days—with milk and sugar? I was an atheist; now I can now believe in God. There is purpose and meaning to existence, and if it was the only way God could go about it, I can even understand and forgive.

But you have three of everything. Is some one going to join us?

Your friend. The one who stormed away! Because on reaching the intersection, your friend will realise that he did not ask, and you did not answer, the last most important question of all—the one that I have for you too. See that person? Running toward us out of fear that you will have left the table, and I will have shut up the sidewalk café for the night.

I will be here for him; I have always been. I know the last question the both of you have for me.

How will it all end?

I am neither a fortune—teller nor a soothsayer. I am certainly not a mystic with divine revelation! To tell you the truth I am not even a science fiction writer and so incapable of seeing worlds within worlds, warped and twisted into 'n' dimensions, with such breath—taking imagination that even God must marvel at their works!

True, we have a little imagination and some little curiosity, and, as common people, we reserve the right to be wrong. We do not have a way with words, so we may have to scratch round for the right ones—and still be unable to express what it is precisely that we want to say.

I am glad this courtroom is empty. The case has been closed—at least for now. It will not be ever finally closed, because there will always be new evidence provided by the astronomers or the paleontologists that demands that we reopen the case. And if there were, we would, unhesitatingly, do just that, because it was never our intention to reach a conclusion, and—in the light of new evidence—be unwilling to change it.

It frees us! The case is closed. Our thoughts can now fly a little. We are not tied to the evidence. What we will now say is right—but just for us! Others may come to different conclusions—and they will be right too. We will all be right, simply because there is no evidence to prove, or disprove, anything we say. We can break the rules of logic; speculate with unashamed abandon. We will discard reason, if we have to. It has been like a corset around us. It will be a relief to loosen the strings and breathe, so that we can be ourselves again.

How will it all end? But first we have to ask ourselves—where have we reached?

Look around you; whatever you see—good or bad—is where we are. We are a work in progress, far from complete, imperfect, but with the more difficult task of putting emotion into elementary particles now a scientific reality! Ask any physicist—or any other scientist for that matter—whether there is any conceivable way in which emotion can be generated, sustained, and enjoyed in inanimate matter and they will drown you with derision! Yet, isn't that exactly what he did? Look around you. Isn't that what has been accomplished by God. He could have sat behind that line of Absolute Zero, if he had chosen to, all alone, knowing all and feeling nothing!

To know and not to feel must have been very sad, and not being able to feel the sadness of it made it sadder still.

How will it all end?

This is an expanding universe. It will, for sure, suffer a heat death. There are already some distant nebulae in our universe that are almost at Absolute Zero in the temperature readings that they transmit to us. The Boomerang Nebula, for example is at a temperature of –272.15°C—just one degree above Absolute Zero. It is only 5000 light—years away from us in the constellation Centaurus.

Nebula?

A vast interstellar cloud composed of gaseous matter, and often luminous.

In many billions of years to come, all the stars in all the galaxies, one by one, will burn themselves up as their fuel gets exhausted. The lights will die out in the sky. The temperature in the entire universe will be near

Absolute Zero.

Why do you keep saying 'almost' Absolute Zero and 'near' Absolute Zero?

Because according to the present Laws of Physics that govern us today, we can never reach Absolute Zero. In a laboratory in Helsinki, we have reached to a few millionths of a degree from Absolute Zero. And the results shatter the Laws of Physics—and sets free our imagination! Matter—the new matter—refuses to obey the law of gravity. When held in a container, the 'Bose-Einstein condensate' climbs up the walls of the container—defying gravity!

Bose—Einstein condensate? Please, do I have to be a physicist again?

The subject was first investigated by an Indian physicist, Satyendra Nath Bose. He wrote a paper, in 1924, and sent it to Einstein who was so impressed that he translated it into German and, under Bose's name, arranged for its publication in a peer—reviewed journal. They worked on atomic behaviour at, or near, Absolute Zero. Einstein published his own work on the subject as well. Atoms made of elementary particles—appropriately named 'bosons', after Bose—showed startling behaviour that defied gravity! When fluids of such bosonic atoms are cooled to near Absolute Zero, the resulting condensate is called a 'Bose-Einstein condensate'—it is, quite simply, 'new' matter.

Fascinating, isn't it? That, when it appears to be the absolute end of the universe, there now appear the New Laws of Physics. Demonstrated in a laboratory in Helsinki.

Here is what I think will happen.

Time will still continue to move forward. We can not reverse time—nor do we want to. But with a new set of the Laws of Physics in place, that will govern the behaviour of the new matter—and the temperature everywhere at, or near, Absolute Zero everywhere—the universe will now start the 'inward' journey to the original center of the 'Big Bang'. Space will start to contract, with the galaxies moving toward each other.

What are these 'new' Laws of Physics?

I haven't a clue! Do you think I'm a physicist? Let them work it out. All I can say is that these new laws will apply only to 'new' inanimate matter—and not to biological organisms, simply because there will be no biological life of any sort whatsoever in the new universe. God will already have acquired the ability to feel. Compassion will have become instinctive; all the base emotions such as anger and hate will have 'evolved' out of our psyche, so that 'good' will finally have triumphed over 'evil'! But some work still remains to be done.

On the outward journey, the key intent was to diversify; on the inward journey, it must be to unify!

I cannot believe that a compassionate and loving God—the sort we believe in and say our prayers to—would permit all the 'injustices' and 'crimes' committed on the outward journey—some of them quite insanely in his name!—to go without being 'righted'. Notice, I did not say 'punished'—just made right again, so that in the vast electronic store of his memory banks of biological organisms over billions of years there is room only for the loving and the joyous. To carry 'evil' or 'hateful' memories would, forever, have the 'knower' of the lamb perpetually afraid of the 'knower' of the lion! We have been considering some bizarre scenarios in the past six days, have we not?

Don't I know!

Well, now that we have abandoned reason itself, our scenarios can be even more bizarre.

Did you see that very pretty woman today—the singer? Or the handsome man on the violin?

Yes, I did.

Did you feel some inner emotion that you might want to be with them? Or, if you fell in love, that you might want to share a life with them? Wouldn't it be an infinitely more joyous an existence, if you were actually 'one' with the other person; if your 'knower' and the other person's 'knower' were the same? Your 'I' and her or his 'I' would be united together, with far more joy than any marriage between the two of you could ever give to either of you? You would be her or him. One with William Shakespeare, or Jane Austen, or Mozart, or Michelangelo; even Moses!

You know, I'm even beginning to like your madness. So I can identify with every biological organism that ever lived—even the family cat.

Precisely! But you would be unable to do that, in full measure, if one of the 'bad' memories you have of the family cat is when she nearly clawed your eyes out as you gave her that foul-tasting medicine recommended by the vet.

Or let us take another scenario. One man murders another in a senseless killing! Perhaps, over a woman.

Or a wife. How could each of the three 'knowers'—the 'I's' of the three of them, conceivably, be able to identify fully with each other—especially the two men, one of whom died—unless the 'wrong' is 'righted'? That will occur when the individual 'knower' realises that it is 'one' with every other 'knower'. Recall we said that the 'knower' was independent of identity. Unification of all 'knowers', with joyous memories has to be the key purpose of the inward journey. Only with this realisation can God then 'tape over' cruel and hateful memories, to erase them from the memory banks, for a joyous existence for all three of them.

There is only the one 'knower'. And the crimes, misdeeds, injustices were committed, not by the 'knower' but by the 'identity' that the 'knower' was associated with at that time. Then, as if with one electronic stroke, all crimes, misdeeds, injustices, merit a compassionate forgiveness, and are erased, because it is we who have committed these wrongs against ourselves. The same applies, of course, to all of the 'crimes' committed by God against us.

Are you going to blaspheme again? His crimes?

A baby dies within six days of birth. Tell me what chance did her 'knower' have to build up the wealth of warm memories of loving parents, of her siblings, of joy and laughter, of the aroma of fresh bread? Don't you think that was so unfair?

You have the answer, of course.

I have 'an' answer. Since the 'knower' is always, and has always been, only one—'echad'—in Hebrew, the 'knower' of that baby has now the opportunity to enjoy any and all of the joyous experiences it was denied in life. Even the experience of growing up, of soccer games, of loving parents, of brothers and sisters, of marriage and babies of her own—all of these experiences are now hers! Because experience is in the final analysis—just memory.

You are talking plain nonsense again! How can all experiences be only 'just' memory? They actually occurred—not just the memory of them!

Tell me, are you enjoying that cup of tea that our host has so graciously given us?

Most certainly. Good Indian tea! Orange pekoe?

Would you be shocked if I were to make the assertion that there is no present—only the past and the future? When the cup reaches your lips—but you have not yet sipped—the 'event' is in the future. When you have sipped, the 'event' is in the past. The future passes through the present into the past. Now, if you were to break down the 'present' into infinitely small micro, micro, micro units of time—say a trillionth of a second—then that unit of time is all that constitutes the 'present'! Before that unit of time, the ‘event’ is in the future—and has not occurred; after that unit of time, the 'event' is in the past—and has been converted into a memory. There really is no ‘present’. Only memories of it. And those can be enjoyed by the child, can they not? God has arranged the passage of time so that all ‘wrongs’—even his own—can be ‘righted’!

I agree with you that ‘wrongs’ have to be ‘righted’. But some of your thinking has rubbed itself off on me. May I be permitted to offer my own scenario for how this can be achieved?

Please do!

Let us say that in the ‘new’ Laws of Physics, that will govern the behaviour of ‘new’ matter, one law on the outward journey is reversed on the inward journey.

The Law of ‘cause’ and ‘effect’. In the New Laws of Physics, whatever was an ‘effect’ in the outward journey becomes the new ‘cause’, and the present ‘cause’ becomes the new ‘effect’. What will then occur is that ‘events’ will be in reverse. Like a video run backward.

No! Definitely not! That would be a serious fallacy in our thinking. When a video is run backward, time is moving backward as well-watch the counter on your VCR, to see what I mean.

All right, if time were still to move forward, but the Laws of Physics, under which the universe operates, are reversed, we would still move ‘forward’, but the 'event' that occurred in the outward journey would be reversed or 'undone'. Because the 'effect' of the 'event' on the outward journey would be the 'cause' on the inward journey, resulting in an 'effect' in the inward journey that was the 'cause' on the outward journey. All as a very natural way to go! For a change, may I ask you: have I lost you?

No. I understand fully.

What this means is that on that inward journey, it will be perfectly 'natural' for the ambulance to pick up the boy and travel to the intersection—reversing the event—then separate from the car, bringing the young woman to life again—reversing the event—then travel to the soccer field and deposit the boy on the ground, who then gets up and resumes the soccer game—reversing the event—until he goes home for his breakfast—reversing the event—since the boy had breakfast before the game and not after it! Birth will consist of a reversal of events at the graveyard with the body coming to life again, while death, that we fear so much, will be the act of gently disappearing into the safety and security of a mother's womb—all as a perfectly natural state of affairs! Any other state of affairs would be considered as freaky and unnatural. Our children's generation will come before ours; we will come before our parent's generation. Do we agree that it is a possible scenario?

Do you recall that at the start of tonight's argument and discussion, I said we could all be right. I cannot, in all conscience, agree with your scenario—and you may disagree with mine—because, in your scenario, the fundamental laws of logic and reason would need reversal as well, for it to work.

For instance?

For instance, the boy went home to have his breakfast, did he not?

Yes. But the events were reversed and the woman is alive!

True. But what did he have for breakfast? Cutlets? Where did that mutton come from? On the outward journey, the goat was butchered, its flesh wrapped into hundreds of little packages—some of them ground up finely into mince meat—that were then sold in the grocery store to hundreds of customers and digested by many hundreds more as chops or cutlets or whatever! How on Earth could you reverse the process on the inward journey—as a natural state of being—thereby ending up once again with a live goat? In simpler terms, if the boy had an egg for breakfast on the outward journey, how do you put humpty—dumpty back together again on the inward one?

I give up! At least until the physicists can tell us more about these 'new' Laws of Physics as they govern the behaviour of 'new' matter. Will biological organisms still need 'biological' food for survival or can we all survive as trees do? Or need no food at all?

But your scenario and mine can be merged into one.

Really?

If we assume that the inward journey, which is for the unification of the 'knowers', takes place with holographic effects—rather than as real events. It has been shown in the laboratory—and demonstrated on television—that holographically any person, or event, can be recreated, for the memory of the event to be erased from the record—or preserved in it—depending on whether it was a 'wrong' that needs to be 'righted', or a 'right' that needs to be preserved for its joyous significance to the players in the event.

I give up as well!

Shall we leave it at that? We can, however, still speculate on the behaviour of inanimate matter?

The galaxies, rushing inward at phenomenal speeds, will gradually build up even more speed and power for the final implosion that will take them to the point from which the outward journey commenced.

In the old laws of Physics, when the temperature of the mass of energy, that was God, was raised from Absolute Zero by a billionth of a degree, the resulting 'explosion' rocketed the temperature to ten billion degrees. Gradually that temperature fell to lower levels where life could begin and be sustained, finally ending in a heat 'death', so that the temperature then fell back to almost Absolute Zero.

In the New Laws of Physics, the 'new' universe, with 'new' matter, is starting at almost Absolute

Zero, with the galaxies now moving toward each other. Eventually that 'new' universe will become more and more dense and compact, and as it does, it will build up enormous pressures—without the corresponding rise in temperatures—but I'm not sure of that!—reverting all matter in the universe to fundamental elementary particles—in which will be stored, electronically, all our memories of good emotions—that he worked so very hard to create—and the ability of a 'knower' to feel them. The New Laws of Physics will then dictate that with all that energy that forms our universe, all concentrated at one point—say the size of an apple—the resulting implosion will drop the temperature of that energy even further, for us to cross the line, once more, to Absolute Zero.

We will have found God.

He will have found us.

We will realise that we have never been apart from him. We have always been him and with him; he has always been us and with us.

[illegible] June [illegible] and tortured police [illegible].

[illegible] regional movement [illegible] ABVP [illegible] student wing of Osmania University [illegible] the [illegible] movement [illegible] communalised [illegible] Muslims of Adilabad district were burnt alive [illegible] a village which is located on the border of Maharashtra [illegible] house in Watoli village, Adilabad district. Nearby Bhainsa town has a communal history and hence government is quite alert. Among those killed in Watoli village are Mehboob Khan, Noman, Arshan, Rizwan, Sahiral Begum and two tender toddler [illegible] Mahesh.

[illegible] July [illegible] Mandal [illegible] opinion of communal violence. A truck carrying [illegible] to hospital [illegible] against some people of the other community and a [illegible] between the two groups belonging to different religions and soon stones flew and properties, shops, houses and vehicles began to burn and firing also took place. The police [illegible] fire. [illegible] escaped by a hair's breadth. In the private firing people were firing from the roofs of their houses. The Police force had [illegible]